Testing the Waters

Testing the Waters

What the Bible Says and Doesn't Say About Baptism

Toby C. Crain

ISBN: 979-8-218-98188-4
Library of Congress Control Number: 2024913688
First Edition

Author's website: https://www.tobycrain.com

Scripture quotations unmarked or marked NIV are taken from the New International Version (NIV), THE HOLY BIBLE, NEW INTERNATIONAL VERSION®, NIV® Copyright © 1973, 1978, 1984, 2011 by Biblica, Inc.® Used by permission. All rights reserved worldwide.

Scripture quotations marked NET are from the NET Bible® Copyright © 1996-2016 by Biblical Studies Press, L.L.C. All rights reserved.

Scripture quotations marked NLT are taken from the Holy Bible, New Living Translation, Copyright © 1996, 2004, 2015 by Tyndale House Foundation. Used by permission of Tyndale House Publishers, Inc., Carol Stream, Illinois 60188. All rights reserved.

Scripture quotations marked NKJV taken from the New King James Version®. Copyright © 1982 by Thomas Nelson. Used by permission. All rights reserved.

Scripture quotations marked NASB taken from the NEW AMERICAN STANDARD BIBLE®, Copyright © 1960, 1962, 1963, 1968, 1971, 1972, 1973, 1975, 1977, 1995 by The Lockman Foundation. Used by permission.

Scripture quotations marked CEB are from the Common English Bible. © Copyright 2011 by the Common English Bible. All rights reserved. Used by permission.

Scripture quotations marked TLV taken from the Tree of Life Version. © 2015 by the Messianic Jewish Family Bible Society. Used by permission of the Messianic Jewish Family Bible Society.

For Zac. You asked the question.
This is the short answer.

Contents

A Gentle Mist

An Introduction

WHY SHOULD WE HAVE a conversation about baptism? Well, maybe you got "baptized" when you were a baby, or as a five-year-old, or perhaps never. It's possible that as an older teen or adult you accepted Jesus and were told you needed to get baptized. Or maybe you weren't.

This leaves a big question mark on our foreheads (among other places) regarding this practice and what it means for us as Christians. Are we really saved if we don't get wet? Are we surely saved because we did? How important is it, really?

Baptism seems to be one of those mysterious Christian concepts that has undergone many changes in understanding, teaching, and implementation over the years. Like other Church doctrines,[1] baptism has been one of those interpretational issues that has led to much discussion and debate over the centuries. Some denominations tell us one thing, and some denominations another.

But what does the Bible say about baptism? Should we, again, just accept what others tell us about this important "sacrament", is it important at all, or should we investigate it ourselves so that we can be without excuse? In my book, *The First Communion: The Making of the Last Supper*, I discussed the importance of understanding the origins of traditions so that we're not ignorant

---

1   **doctrine** (*dok´ trin*)—*a particular principle, position, or policy taught or advocated, as of a religion or government.* Doctrine stems from the Latin *doctrina*, from the root *docere*, meaning to teach. "Doctor" shares this same root.

and, as such, are not deceived. We must also not put too much weight on what we "think" or "feel" is right since these are unreliable sources.

> *The heart is deceitful above all things and beyond cure. Who can understand it?*
>
> JEREMIAH **17:9 NIV**

> *The* LORD *knows people's thoughts; he knows they are worthless!*
>
> PSALM **94:11 NLT**

> *I have always tried my best to let wisdom guide my thoughts and actions. I said to myself, "I am determined to be wise." But it didn't work.*
>
> ECCLESIASTES **7:23 NLT**

Not to diminish the talents and education of Christian teachers, scholars and pastors, but we must also not lean too heavily on what others tell us, read on the internet, or hear from the pulpit. Since God has given us the ability to learn and understand directly from His Word, no special knowledge or education is required.

While the New Testament mentions baptism quite a bit—even providing a few examples—its earliest practices were still misunderstood by the generations of Christians following the turn of the first century.

As we'll discuss later, the concept of ritual washing by immersion (baptism) was already a Jewish practice. And though this idea of ceremonial washing was not unique to Jews, the non-Jewish or *Gentile* Christian community didn't fully understand it, and simply acted in obedience to Jesus:

> *"All authority in heaven has been given to me. Therefore go and make disciples of all nations, baptizing them in the name of the Father and of the Son and of the Holy Spirit, and teaching them to obey everything I have commanded you. And surely I am with you always, to the very end of the age."*
>
> MATTHEW 28:18-20 NIV

So new believers, or disciples, got baptized—as they were instructed—as soon after conversion as possible. They did this to keep in step with Jesus' example and directive, and to continue in expected obedience. At least that's how it appears.

This was documented throughout the New Testament book of Acts (frequently referred to as the Acts of the Apostles or the Acts of the Holy Spirit) which bore witness to all subsequent generations that this demonstration of faith was important. We'll later note that conversion was always a process, as one is never born a Christian, though one most certainly must be born again.

Of course, new disciples, as noted within the book of Acts, *didn't have* the book of Acts to draw upon. Instead, they responded directly to the Good News by getting baptized. In chapter eight of Acts, we see the apostle Philip interacting with a man from Ethiopia who had been reading about the coming messiah in Isaiah 53:

> *The [Ethiopian] eunuch asked Philip, "Tell me, please, who is the prophet talking about, himself or someone else?" Then Philip began with that very passage of Scripture and told him the good news about Jesus.*
>
> *As they traveled along the road, they came to some water and the eunuch said, "Look, here is water. What can stand in the way of my being baptized?" And he gave orders to stop the chariot. Then both Philip and the eunuch went down into the water and Philip baptized him.*
>
> ACTS 8:34-38 NIV

Why would the eunuch demand to be baptized if Philip had not included the directive to do so when sharing the Good News with him? But as we'll see, things changed from early on. Even though baptism was originally performed by immersion (completely underwater, as that's the meaning of the Greek word *baptisma*), later generations of Christian church leaders began discussing this necessity. Many suggested that only partial wetness was needed, and that just a simple pouring or sprinkling of water on the recipient was sufficient.

There even came a time when new believers were required to "prove" their conversion beforehand, having to then wait until Easter Sunday to be permitted to get baptized! Harvey Albert Smit tells us:

> Around A.D. 150 Christians generally agreed that becoming a Christian involved three stages. The first stage was an initial assent to the faith—what we would call today "accepting Christ as your personal Savior." The second stage was a probationary period during which the new believer was expected to show the sincerity of his or her new faith by a real change in life patterns. Justin Martyr delineates three requirements for this stage: sorrow for sin, learning and accepting the church's teachings, and transforming one's life. The third stage was the baptismal period: believers were required to fast and pray for several days before Easter and were baptized on Easter morning.[2]

All these different philosophies contributed to the doctrinal differences that led to the splitting of the early Church and into the various denominations that have sprouted up over the

---

2   *Easter Baptism: An Ancient Tradition.* Harvey Albert Smit (March 1987), Worship Ministries of the Christian Reformed Church. https://www.reformedworship.org/

centuries (though there aren't as many as you may have heard).

Unless you're a brand-new believer—or the church you grew up in doesn't practice it at all—it's quite likely that you already have a general understanding of baptism. You may even have already formed your own opinion about it and whether it's very important in accomplishing anything at all (especially since there's no soap involved).

Like you, I have my own opinions about it. I won't share those with you, obviously, as that would bias this discussion. But I *can* tell you that, as a youth, I was originally taught one thing (and though I've forgotten what it was by now, I've since learned many other things) and then—after coming to faith in Jesus as an adult and having grown up in Christ, I began to see that this subject of baptism wasn't as wet and dried as everyone seemed to make it. There were questions and inconsistencies, and so I inadvertently found fault with anyone who stood too firmly in their position.

Many today contend that baptism is a requirement for salvation, while others say it's only a symbolic gesture and therefore, while important, unnecessary. The simple fact that Christians can take different positions on this subject is a clear indicator to me that there's more going on here than what we may see on the surface.

As we immerse ourselves in this subject, we'll try to be respectful of everyone's understanding of this practice (excluding those who don't yet understand it) while diving in with eyes open to the possibility that what we think we know may be partially obscured by the muddy waters around us. We won't know for sure until we get in, so I can't make any claims one way or another. We'll need to hold our collective breath at times and dive deep. But together, in the safety of our literary bathyspheres, we'll search the Scriptures to discover the truth and bring it to the surface.

Throughout this discussion and investigation, I will assume that you are not a biblical scholar, and so I'll try to avoid any excessive and superfluous vocabulary. I believe it's of paramount importance that this symposium remains relevant and contemporaneous, and I will be vigilant in my endeavor to avoid being a haughty raconteur.

But obviously, if you are a biblical scholar, you won't be very open to anything we'll be talking about here anyway; so, you can just go ahead and stick this book back on the shelf, or perhaps under one of the legs of your coffee table to keep it level.

As always (and when I say "always" I mean this is only the second time), I would like to point out a couple of things before we get started. First, I will make a genuine effort to capitalize any pronouns or references to any member of the Trinity (the Father, the Son, or the Holy Spirit) such as *He, Him, or His* (there may be others, but I can't think of Them right now). And I do this just to clearly distinguish Him from any other lesser pronouns rushing in and trying to get unwarranted attention.

Also (this would be the second thing) I'd like to mention that we'll be looking at a lot of biblical text during our investigation. To make it easy for us, I'll include those references (as many as are legally allowed) right in these pages. Not only does it make my book appear larger, it has the added benefit of allowing you to read along without having to carry around your own Bible.

This is very important to me because I know the Bible can get pretty heavy and I don't want it to weigh you down. Life can get rather heavy on its own. I also want you to know that I'm not making anything up (certainly nothing you can prove). We'll reach conclusions together based on the biblical text that we read together. And while you will have the freedom (in Christ) to reach different conclusions, I'll ask that you write them down so that you can include them in your own book when you're ready.

When I do provide such passages for discussion, we'll look at different translations so that we can enjoy the new perspectives that can sometimes develop when doing so. As we run this race, however (Hebrews 12:1), it's important that you do reference your own Bible from time to time so that you can fact-check me and make sure I stay in my lane and not get disqualified.

And the people of Berea were more open-minded than those in Thessalonica, and they listened eagerly to Paul's message. They searched the Scriptures day after day to see if Paul and Silas were teaching the truth.

Acts 17:11 NLT

Lastly (I guess there were three things), I will differentiate between *Church* and *church*. This means that whenever we're referencing the establishment of the Church—such as the Christian Church as one body, or the institution of a particular denomination, such as the Roman Catholic or Methodist Church (even though we won't have any good reason to talk about the Methodist Church)—Church will be capitalized, whether you like it or not. However, when we're just talking about your local church or congregation—which is clearly not as important—we won't capitalize it. Therefore, we're either referring to "The Church" or we're referring to "a church." You get it?

Now, while I've consulted a number of books and commentaries on this subject of baptism over the years, I found that none of them seemed to be particularly objective. Each and every one started with a presupposition according to which the author or "teacher" carefully examined and "proved" his preconceived points.

The work before you is an effort at doing exactly the opposite. We will read the Bible together and see what it says without trying to read our presumptions into it.

If this idea appeals to you, then I would like to officially invite you to investigate this topic with me as we take a closer look at the origins and history of baptism to see if we can't find out together if any of this really matters at all.

Diving In
Chapter 1: Defining Baptism

So what is baptism anyway? We've all heard of water baptism, baptism by fire, and baptism of the Holy Spirit. And most of us understand that baptism, in some way, means to get wet—usually in connection with being a Christian. But how exactly?

If you grew up anywhere in the Church, you should already have an idea of what baptism is all about. Shouldn't you? The trouble, however, is that baptism can mean a lot of different things to a lot of different people, both in the Church and out. Believers raised in a more orthodox home (Roman Catholic, Eastern Orthodox, Anglican, etc.) have a completely different understanding of baptism than those from a Baptist or Methodist background (oops, there it is!), and perhaps different again from a variety of other Protestant and evangelical perspectives.

These perspectives or understandings are based almost entirely on what those in our own churches have taught or told us . . . or not. There are congregations out there that believe baptism is a much ado about nothing, and they forgo it altogether. This forces us to raise the question as to why there are different understandings and teachings regarding baptism at all? **If Jesus modeled it and commanded us to do it, why has it become so complicated?**

"Therefore, go and make disciples of all the nations, baptizing them in the name of the Father and the Son and the Holy Spirit. Teach these new disciples to obey all the commands I have given you."
Matthew 28:19-20 NIV

Having been immersed in a Catholic childhood originally and then sprinkled a bit in the Lutheran and Baptist cultures, I eventually waded out into the deeper waters of the evangelical community (or perhaps they weren't as deep, and I just got shorter). The main advantage of this later stage, I guess, is that it afforded me the opportunity to dig into the Bible myself to learn the truth of things instead of relying solely on the teachings of various church leaders.

With this in mind, since I myself have carefully investigated everything from the beginning, I too decided to write an orderly account for you, most excellent Theophilus, so that you may know the certainty of the things you have been taught.
Luke 1:3-4 NIV

This point is two-fold. First is the reality that I had pulled away from the *structure* of Big Church which allowed me to actually open up my Bible and read it, and not just have it read or recited *to me* out of context. Second is that as I grew more mature in my faith (I did! I did! I did!) and as I read my Bible more deeply and more frequently, I came to find that many of the things I grew up believing or understanding just were not true (or at least not biblically supported).

This sparked in me a desire to step even deeper into the mist to discover the truth I sought. Tragically for some, such doubts or discoveries can cause them to throw their hands up in disgust and say, "It's all a big lie!" and then walk away from God.

> *At this, many of his disciples turned away and no longer accompanied him. Jesus asked the Twelve, "Do you also want to leave?" Simon Peter answered, "Lord, where would we go? You have the words of eternal life."*
>
> JOHN 6:66-68 CEB

Instead, I steered more deeply into God and His Word to learn the truth from the source. As an adult, I could see that people had historically made some honest mistakes, made some decisions, and allowed pride or ignorance to rule those choices. And in most cases, the untruths I had been hearing from the pulpit didn't even originate there, but rather from centuries of misunderstandings and the "blind leading the blind" (Luke 6:39).

Now don't get me wrong, for we must certainly hold up our pastors, priests, and other "men of God" (and women) in the leadership positions to which they have been placed, whether by God or by men (or women). But these men (and women)[3] are still just sin-filled individuals who must fulfill their responsibilities amidst the chaos created by their sin-filled spouses, children, friends, and extended families. And when the pride of an elevated position is given permission to flourish, anything can happen. Even for priests and others who (vow to) remain celibate and live without a wife and kids, are they not themselves children? Do they not themselves have families or other blood relatives? And of course, the very role of leadership itself is fraught with corporate politics and turmoil, regardless of the greater body to which they belong.

And just a quick reminder: *you too are a sinner!* Sorry to break it to you. But if you call yourself a child of God then you are most certainly sin-filled. Yes, Jesus is the "Lamb of God who takes away the sins of the world" and who makes it possible for us to approach God's throne. But that "taking away" was not the

---

3 *"Why don't you shut up about women, Stan, you're putting us off!"* from Monty Python's Life of Brian. Handmade Films; Python (Monty) Pictures Ltd. (1979)

expulsion of sin from our bodies, but rather the "washing" of our souls through the purification of His blood in order that God would not see our sin and hold it against us.

> *If we claim to have fellowship with him and yet walk in the darkness, we lie and do not live out the truth. But if we walk in the light, as he is in the light, we have fellowship with one another, and the blood of Jesus, his Son, purifies us from all sin. If we claim to be without sin, we deceive ourselves and the truth is not in us. If we confess our sins, he is faithful and just and will forgive us our sins and purify us from all unrighteousness. If we claim we have not sinned, we make him out to be a liar and his word is not in us.*
>
> 1 JOHN 1:6-10 NIV

> *For there is no distinction; for all have sinned and fall short of the glory of God, being justified as a gift by His grace through the redemption which is in Christ Jesus.*
>
> ROMANS 3:2-24 NASB

This is the Good News! When we hear or speak about "accepting Jesus" we're talking about accepting Christ's atoning sacrifice for us, and we are acknowledging—through profession or confession—that we are sinful and unclean, and that "while we were still sinners, Christ died for us" (Romans 5:8). Because we are sinful "by nature" there is no need for us to first live a life of sin to be eligible for forgiveness. In the moment we are brought into this world (at conception), which is corrupted, our bodies have also already been corrupted.

And while we may argue the age at which one might be held accountable for his sin, there is no argument that we have sinned, and so we certainly require Jesus' blood to make atonement for us. But while His blood is made available for us to be used for that atonement (so that we don't have to use our own), it is offered to us as a gift with no strings attached. This would suggest that there is nothing more that must be physically done by us in exchange for this gift. There is no pay back for God's gift. If this were a wage, then God would demand some kind of work in return for it. But while "the payoff of sin is death; the gift of God is eternal life in Christ Jesus our Lord" (Romans 6:23 NET). However, it's imperative to understand that this gift can *only* be accepted by faith. For only when we believe in the power of Jesus' blood to make us right with God can it actively do so. And so, accepting Jesus is believing in and accepting this free gift.

But here's the caveat: if you grew up in the Church and simply just "believed that" Jesus died for you, that's not the same as "trusting in" Jesus as a response to the Gospel. A response is what the Ethiopian eunuch experienced mentioned earlier, and as did over three thousand men who accepted Peter's message and were baptized on the day of Pentecost (Acts 2:14-39).

DOES BAPTISM SAVE YOU?

This really is the big question, isn't it? I mean, every single doctrine and practice of baptism boil down to the belief of the answer to this question. But because that belief changed over time as the presence and instruction of the original apostles themselves faded, the process and purpose of baptism also changed over that time. Some came to believe that the act of baptism itself is the "moment" of salvation. In Acts 2:38, Peter says to his audience, "repent and be baptized . . . and you will receive the gift of the Holy Spirit." Would this also mean that one receives the Holy Spirit at baptism? When Jesus was baptized, John (the Baptizer) saw "the Spirit of God descending on him like a dove" (Matthew 3:16).

But if we could equate the idea of being born again with our physical birth, we might ask, "When does life begin?" And as it's a scientific consensus that life begins at the moment of conception,[4]

---

4   *The Scientific Consensus on When a Human's Life Begins.* National Institutes of Health, National Library of Medicine. https://pubmed.ncbi.nlm.nih.gov/36629778/

we could postulate that a new life begins at the "reception" of Jesus as Lord and Savior. Following this same thought then, baptism would seem equivalent to being physically born by leaving the mother's womb, be it via the birth canal or via medical assistance or intervention.

Some contend that the act of baptism supplements the atoning work of Christ on the cross and finishes the job. Citing that same passage from Acts above, there's an indication that the Holy Spirit does not come until baptism, not just upon faith in Jesus. But certainly, there must be more going on here (more on this later) since we can read of a circumstance where believers received the Holy Spirit before baptism:

> *While Peter was still speaking these words, the Holy Spirit came on all who heard the message … Then Peter said, "Surely no one can stand in the way of their being baptized with water. They have received the Holy Spirit just as we have." So he ordered that they be baptized in the name of Jesus Christ.*
> Acts 10:44, 47-48 NIV

Here, Peter "ordered" that they be baptized! While many believe that baptism is simply a symbolic and unnecessary gesture, like a "statement of faith", there are others still who believe that baptism is more akin to a wedding ceremony completed only when the groom slides a ring onto the finger of his bride. Not just a statement of faith, but an act of public declaration, with witnesses and everything.

In fact, as early as the fourth century, it became a common practice to delay baptism into adulthood because of the belief that baptism actually performs the cleansing of sin (and is therefore part of the salvation process).

Andrew Koperski tells us:

> The early Christian habit of hyper-delayed baptism is well attested by the later fourth century. Apparently, the

reasoning behind waiting until fairly late in life was that baptism cleansed sin once and only once. Consequently, any meaningful sin after baptism could leave one in a serious lurch in the economy of salvation. Earlier in the fourth century, Constantine himself had delayed baptism to his deathbed.[5]

Today, there are seemingly good arguments for each position of this discussion, and the fact that there is an argument indicates differences in understanding of the biblical texts. There seem to be passages that "say" one thing, and then other passages that appear to "say" something else. So, it will take a bit of effort to put those pieces together to see the coherent picture God has given us.

Therefore, we need to approach this initial question with a little bit of care (remember, there's no running around the pool). So, let's begin by stepping back for a moment and asking, *If Jesus hadn't died and been raised from the dead, then what exactly would my faith be about?*

If you confess with your mouth Jesus as Lord, and believe in your heart that God raised Him from the dead, you will be saved; for with the heart a person believes, resulting in righteousness, and with the mouth he confesses, resulting in salvation.

ROMANS 10:9 10 NASB

And if Christ has not been raised, your faith is futile; you are still in your sins.

1 CORINTHIANS 15:17 NIV

If Jesus hadn't died, been buried, and raised to new life, would my baptism accomplish anything? Certainly not, it would have

---

5   *Baptismal Trajectories in Early Christianity, Part III: Toward an Explanation.* Andrew Koperski (Feb 2022). https://adfontesjournal.com/church-history/baptismal-trajectories-in-early-christianity-part-iii-toward-an-explanation/

no value at all! It has value only because He did die and was most assuredly raised from the dead. But then the follow-up question is, *Does the act of getting baptized "complete" in me what Jesus started?* Was the work that He did somehow insufficient for me?

Let's ask it a different way. If God was willing to send His one and only Son to die for me (while I was still a hot mess, I must add), should I even consider that He would rely on my "righteousness" to finish the job? I just can't see it. But if so, would such righteousness kick in before or after my baptism? Did I do it right? Did I say the right words? What if I missed a spot?

You see, those are the implications of such positions and the very reasons there are disagreements, and, hence, why we're talking about it. So let's cast off any preconceptions we have about it and instead take the road less traveled.

Rain, Waterfall, and a River
Chapter 2: Methods of Baptism

THERE ARE A NUMBER of different ways in which an individual might get baptized. Specifically, there are three different methods of baptism used in (or out of) Christian churches across the globe. Of course, each of these methods, in and of themselves, we can all agree (even though we won't) accomplish nothing but getting one wet. For without faith, the action is meaningless:

> *Now without faith it is impossible to please him, for the one who approaches God must believe that he exists and that he rewards those who seek him.*
> HEBREWS 11:6 NET

> *As the body without the spirit is dead, so faith without deeds is dead.*
> JAMES 2:26 NIV

Immersion

Immersion baptism involves an individual being partially or completely "submerged" in water. This is typically performed in a body of water in which the one to be baptized stands in the water with another individual who is "performing" the baptism. As is customary, but which varies by implementation, words are spoken to witnesses in attendance, often followed by a "profession of faith" (in accordance with Romans 10:9-10 noted previously), finishing with the individual's immediate and complete, though momentary, submersion into the water, as he or she is again brought back up to a standing position (and sometimes a standing ovation) and a "new life."

This method is most closely linked to the Jewish practice of the ceremonial *mikveh (mik-vay')*, as we'll discuss later, which is why Jean le Baptiste dunked his disciples in the Jordan River. This was then repurposed by Jesus, now with much greater significance, and was the method used to baptize all new believers throughout the first century.

Affusion

Affusion is the pouring of water onto the individual's head. This may have been occasionally performed in places where there were insufficient bodies of water available to practice immersion. This may have also been applicable to the old or infirm (or imprisoned) who were physically unable to travel as needed to receive it. Today, this method is most often used for infants in churches where their baptism or, more appropriately, "dedication" is practiced. Those churches that baptize by affusion typically don't deny the legitimacy of baptism by immersion, but have determined, in accordance with Church history, that affusion is sufficient for the purpose.

That history took its lead from a brief anonymous document called *The Teaching of the Twelve Apostles* which is commonly referred to as the *Didache* (literally "teaching"). Dated to the late first or early second century, it contains some early (though inadequate) direction regarding apostolic teachings, sort of like the first Church manual. Because of its style, composition and anonymity, it was undetermined whether or not it truly came from an apostolic source and was therefore not included in the biblical canon of the New Testament, even though it was still used as a reference by subsequent generations.

In it we find:

> But if you have no living water, baptize into other water;
> and if you cannot do so in cold water, do so in warm water.
> But if you have neither, pour out water three times upon the
> head into the name of Father and Son and Holy Spirit.
> —*Didache, VII, 2-3* [6]

And while there are no examples of baptism by affusion in the New Testament, or of any parallel implementation of "washing" in the Old Testament, it was at least a method that was likely in use by the end of the second century.

Aspersion

The sprinkling of water on the recipient is another method of baptism. In some churches, aspersion is often accomplished using an *aspergillum* (a knob at the end of a stick, technically speaking). This instrument is used so that the church official doesn't have to get his hands wet. (Do you see what I did there, Pontius?)

As noted earlier, on the Jewish holiday of Pentecost there were over three thousand conversions. But years afterward, some folks became convinced that it would have been impossible for so many people to have undergone immersion baptism at one time. [7] So they concluded that either affusion or aspersion must have been used in that instance. Of course, the flaw in that argument is that the additional instruments necessary to perform such sprinkling wouldn't have been available to expedite the process. In either case, you know what they say happens when you *asperse* something . . .

Now, it seemed for many, then and now, that "sprinkling" didn't quite do the trick for many in the Christian community,

---

6   *The Didache.* http://www.thedidache.com

7   *3000 Baptisms.* Scot McKnight (February 2020). https://www.christianitytoday.com/scot-mcknight/2020/february/3000-baptisms-but-where-in-jerusalem.html

and this doubt caused concern and controversy. But this concern seems valid only when one believes that the waters of baptism *are* waters of salvation.

Because of this, one of the early Church leaders, Cyprian, penned this response in a letter to a young man named Magnus:

> You have asked also, dearest son, what I thought of those who obtain God's grace in sickness and weakness, whether they are to be accounted legitimate Christians, for that they are not to be washed, but sprinkled, with the saving water . . . I think that the divine benefits can in no respect be mutilated and weakened; nor can anything less occur in that case, where, with full and entire faith both of the giver and receiver, is accepted what is drawn from the divine gifts . . . nor ought it to trouble any one that sick people seem to be sprinkled or affused, when they obtain the Lord's grace, when Holy Scripture speaks by the mouth of the prophet Ezekiel, and says, "Then will I sprinkle clean water upon you . . ." (Ezekiel 36:25) . . . Whence it appears that the sprinkling also of water prevails equally with the washing of salvation; and that when this is done in the Church, where the faith both of receiver and giver is sound, all things hold and may be consummated and perfected by the majesty of the Lord and by the truth of faith.
> —*Cyprian, Epistle 75, 12* [8]

If Cyprian, in the third century, was already considering the "saving water" of baptism, it was obviously well-established that this was an accepted idea among many. Remarkably, Cyprian takes it a step further to indicate that by Christ's own words, only other believers "who have the Holy Spirit" can forgive the sins of another:

---

8   *Cyprian Epistle 75.* Translated by Robert Ernest Wallis. From Ante-Nicene Fathers, Vol. 5. Edited by Alexander Roberts, James Donaldson, and A. Cleveland Coxe. (Buffalo, NY: Christian Literature Publishing Co., 1886.) Revised and edited for New Advent by Kevin Knight. http://www.newadvent.org/fathers/050675.htm

For since in baptism everyone has his own sins remitted, the Lord proves and declares in His Gospel that sins can only be put away by those who have the Holy Spirit . . . "As the Father has sent me, even so send I you." And when He had said this, He breathed on them, and said to them, "Receive the Holy Ghost. Whose soever sins you remit, they shall be remitted unto them; and whose soever sins you retain, they shall be retained" (John 20:21-23). In which place He shows that he alone can baptize and give remission of sins who has the Holy Spirit.
—*Cyprian, Epistle 75, 11*

This began (or affirmed) the idea that Christian men held the power to forgive sins on earth. However, what Jesus meant (in the referenced passage of John 20:21-13) was that He was sending His disciples (and by extension, us) to take the Good News to the whole world. **Jesus was leaving them physically, but promised He would remain with them as the Holy Spirit.** So that as the disciples went out to proclaim the gospel, they could honestly tell people who believed in Jesus that their sins were forgiven, while likewise telling those that did not believe that their sins would not be forgiven and that they already stood condemned in God's eyes. Just as Jesus said,

> *"Anyone who believes in God's Son has eternal life. Anyone who doesn't obey the Son will never experience eternal life but remains under God's angry judgment."*
> JOHN 3:36 NLT

Besides, we know that only God can forgive sins.

> *"Why does this fellow talk like that? He's blaspheming! Who can forgive sins but God alone?"*
> MARK 2:7 NIV

Unfortunately, this kind of thinking was pervasive in the Church by that time, and it was believed that since men in the priesthood (or clergy) held the power of forgiveness, they could offer or refuse baptism to anyone. This included infants, of course, and there were many discussions regarding this as well. Ultimately, Cyprian affirmed this practice too, since it was (and is) understood that newborns also carry the default guilt of Adam's sin. Says King David:

> *Look, I was guilty of sin from birth, a sinner the moment my mother conceived me.*
> PSALM 51:5 NET

Ironically, not everyone accepts the teaching of original sin even though it's right there in the Bible. Regardless, many believe that children mustn't be held accountable for their sins until they are old enough—typically around the age of adolescence (12 or 13), coinciding with the Jewish tradition of *bat-* or *bar-mitzvah* (meaning "child of the law")—though oftentimes much earlier.

But in the Roman Catholic Church, it became doctrine that baptism was integral to the process of salvation, and so everyone was at risk of never receiving (or losing) theirs. This remains problematic for infants (or anyone) who die before baptism, or for any child or adult who, having once been baptized, might possibly sin again before they die (however unlikely that may be).

The way I read it, however, the Bible plainly tell us that Jesus "takes away the sins of the world" (John 1:29). And while all mankind was once guilty as a result of Adam's sin, so too is all mankind now justified (though not saved) by Christ's sacrifice.

> *Consequently, just as one trespass resulted in condemnation for all people, so also one righteous act resulted in justification and life for all people.*
> ROMANS 5:18 NIV

This means that our sin cannot be "washed away" through the waters of baptism, because it has already been "taken away" by Jesus' sacrifice on the cross. That sacrifice removed the barrier between us and God so that we are free to choose to accept or reject Him without excuse. And so that when we do believe, the Bible says we are saved. This is because salvation comes from God through our faith in Jesus Christ, not through the power of getting ourselves wet.

> *It is the power of God that brings salvation to everyone who believes.*
> Romans 1:16 NIV

Therefore, baptism must do or mean something else. Again, there's room for disagreement here, but we must first always ask where and how the doctrine we personally hold to was first established. Did it come from our own reading and interpretation of Scripture, or did someone else tell us what to believe?

Clearly there's more going on here; so for now, let's just acknowledge how these variances in the practice of baptism came into being. And as we move forward to agree with one another in completely different ways, let us boldly encounter these different perspectives to see where it takes us.

The Old Is Gone
Chapter 3: A Flood of Changes

LET'S TAKE A LOOK NOW at how all this baptism stuff got started. For this, we need to go all the way back to the Old Testament, back to the earliest pages of the book of Genesis.

> *The LORD observed the extent of human wickedness on the earth, and he saw that everything they thought or imagined was consistently and totally evil. So the LORD was sorry he had ever made them and put them on the earth. It broke his heart. And the LORD said, "I will wipe this human race I have created from the face of the earth. Yes, and I will destroy every living thing—all the people, the large animals, the small animals that scurry along the ground, and even the birds of the sky. I am sorry I ever made them." But Noah found favor with the LORD.*
>
> GENESIS 6:5-8 NLT

Enough was enough, God decided. It was time for a change. While the book of Genesis doesn't record the year in which the earth and the rest of the universe was created, we do know a few years had passed before Noah came on the scene.

If you're a young-earth Creationist,[9] like the Orthodox Jew, you believe that Adam and Eve got bored of their lives in Eden rather quickly, got the Divine Boot, and started having kids. The genealogies in Genesis 5 then help us calculate the "starting

---

9   *Is Genesis History?* Compass Cinema (2017). https://isgenesishistory.com/

point" of the earth's clock, and the calendar starts from there (not to put too fine a point on it) at 3761 BCE.[10]

Now, be mindful that the calendar designations the world uses—separating BC (before Christ) from AD (Latin *anno domini,* or "year of the lord")—didn't exist at the time of Christ. In those days, folks simply referenced the date as it was related to the current ruler in a specific region (since they were speaking or writing to a typically local audience). And this was only for historical purposes, since people generally lived in the present. Nobody had to worry about writing down the date all the time on their classroom papers or on a bank check, and they didn't need to get used to writing the digit change for the first couple of weeks every year.

For example, Luke records the year in which Jesus was born:[11]

> *In those days Caesar Augustus issued a decree that a census should be taken of the entire Roman world. (This was the first census that took place while Quirinius was governor of Syria.) And everyone went to their own town to register.*
> Luke 2:1-3 NIV

And in the chapter that follows, Luke records the year in which John the Baptizer (Jesus' cousin) begins His public ministry:

> *In the fifteenth year of the reign of Tiberius Caesar—when Pontius Pilate was governor of Judea, Herod tetrarch of Galilee, his brother Philip tetrarch of Iturea and Traconitis, and Lysanias tetrarch of Abilene—during the high-priesthood of Annas and*

---

10   BCE—*before the common era.* Many today who use the contemporary or *Gregorian* calendar (introduced by Pope Gregory VIII in 1582), in a desire to exclude Christ from the dating system and make the dating system more generic, recently re-introduced the designations of CE *(The Common Era)* and BCE *(Before the Common Era)*—first used in the sixth century (though I can't remember if it was AD or CE)—as alternates to the BC and AD abbreviations we are all familiar with. In either case, it's remarkable to note that Jesus was probably born AD.

11   *Was There Really a Census During the Time of Caesar Augustus?* Krista Wenzel (December 2014). https://crossexamined.org/really-census-time-caesar-augustus/

Caiaphas, the word of God came to John son of Zechariah in the wilderness. He went into all the country around the Jordan, preaching a baptism of repentance for the forgiveness of sins.

Luke 3:1-3 NIV

In this way, Luke is recalling a very specific year, noting not just one ruler, but seven different rulers converging on history at the same point in time. Now the people and places recorded by Luke have been a source of controversy for many scholars who, until recently, had been unable to verify any of these things, with arguments arising over the year of the beginning of Tiberius Caesar's reign. But recent archaeological discoveries have helped to validate these things,[12] as well as many others that demonstrate the accuracy of the Bible's historical basis.

But Luke was clearly writing to a contemporary audience, and they would have immediately known whether his "facts" were bogus or not since his gospel was likely written within fifteen to twenty years of the Resurrection. And logically, if Luke was just trying to spin some fantastic yarn of his own making, why in the world would he intentionally pollute it with such easily fact-checkable details?

As I was saying, years were typically reckoned by a ruler's reign. In the same way, we might remember "the seventh year of Ronald Reagan's presidency." In that year, among many other notable events, the world experienced the disastrous post-launch explosion of the Space Shuttle *Challenger* as well as the catastrophic meltdown of the Soviet nuclear power plant *Chernobyl*. Because Reagan began his first term in 1980, we know with certainty that these events took place in 1986 (AD or CE, depending on your perspective).

So, as we look back at the Hebrew calendar, we find that the event of Creation took place on the first day of the first month of

---

12   *What Was the Fifteenth Year of Tiberius?* Associates for Biblical Research.
https://biblearchaeology.org/research/the-daniel-9-24-27-project/4363-what-was-the-fifteenth-year-of-tiberius

the first year, which puts us really darn close to the six-thousand year mark (if you believe such things, of course). But since there was no way with which to measure the time that elapsed between verses two and three of Genesis—nor is it recorded how much time passed between Adam's and Eve's introduction to the Garden on Day Six and their subsequent expulsion—we can't know if their recorded lifespans actually include their ages prior to the Fall. As a result, we are left with the true year of Creation a debatable mystery . . . for now.

OH! THE PAIN

Reading ahead to Genesis chapter five we discover that Adam, Eve, and most of their immediate descendants lived for nearly a thousand years each. I think it's reasonable to assume that Eve had given birth to a few kids before leaving the Garden. God's remark that He would significantly "increase her pain" in childbirth (Genesis 3:16) supports this reasoning. For if she hadn't yet given birth, God's words wouldn't mean anything to her. If she had yet to experience nine months of pregnancy and the physical birth of a child, it would have been a very hollow curse.

And so, we should expect that they had already been in the kid-making business for quite a while before being cast out of the Garden. Besides, during their time in Eden, they were eternal. They ate from the Tree of Life and would not die. Why should any measurement of time be ascribed to them at all?

But for fun, let's just consider that they had lived only a hundred years in the Garden before being cast out. As I know there are couples who have had ten or twelve kids within a span of only twenty years (though they usually stop by the time they're forty), it seems fair to assume that the First Parents had at least fifty to eighty kids during their time in the Garden since they were commanded from the get-go to "be fruitful and multiply" (Genesis 1:28)—and then perhaps another fifty kids each and every hundred years after that.

In an earlier work, I noted that in only about two hundred years the seventy members of the family of Israel (Exodus 1:5) could have grown to a number exceeding 2.4 million.[13] This means that, in our present discussion, these "Genesis 3" families would have continued growing and spreading out across the countryside; and it was likely that many of them traveled great distances over time. Over the span of the next thousand years, of course, we could reasonably expect folks to have traveled to the far reaches of the continents. This could have been as far north as Britain, as far east as the Far East, and as far south as the ends of Africa—even *Out of Africa.*

It's even possible, and likely, that people had traveled across the Alaskan peninsula from Asia into the North American continent and then south (except in those days I think that area was called India). And certainly, before the Flood, only God knows what the land masses looked like.

Now, having set the stage for what happened after Adam and Eve prematurely left the Garden, we try to imagine the reality of the world that would have existed after a really long time of making babies (everybody was doing it in those days) and experiencing only occasional death (since natural causes took a while). Instead of just a small, localized community, we can expect that the entire earth likely had scattered inhabitants throughout.

And it's not a big leap to accept that, as corrupt as the world was according to God's perspective, there was plenty of mischief, mayhem and murder across all of Adam's clans.

But as we look at the written account of Adam's line of descendants all the way down to Noah (we're still looking at Genesis 5), each of whom lives seven to nine hundred years of age, we note that they all had other sons and daughters (while also noting that the son highlighted was not necessarily the first

---

13   *The First Communion: The Making of the Last Supper.* Toby C. Crain (June 2022)

born).

We then read through those one thousand and fifty years to when Noah was born, ten generations later. Chapter 5 then ends by jumping ahead another five hundred years to some point after Noah's wife *Emzara*[14] bore him three sons (not all at once): Shem, Ham, and Japheth.

Seeing that Noah's generation lived ten times longer than humans do today, we should regard his six-hundredth year as something relative to his fiftieth birthday (based on a man's average lifespan today), and not discount Noah as a decrepit old man too advanced for children. If Noah and his wife had the strength to spend the next half-century or more building that big boat, they surely had the energy to raise a few wily kids.

As we discussed with Adam and Eve (well, not with them, but in regard to them), it's not very likely that Noah and his wife went a full five hundred years without having any kids, as there's no indication that she was barren. But even if they did, any other children—with all their families and descendants—would have been lost in the obscurity of the world and the corruption that had come anyway, and there'd be no reason to mention them. So forget I brought it up.

WASHED AWAY

God decided to start again. Having already contended with His disappointment of Adam and Eve a millennia before, He'd put into play the script for the salvation and redemption of all humankind. God waited for Noah to be born—since Noah had already been chosen—so that He could begin laying the groundwork for His master plan (though I admit the concept of God waiting is tough for me to noodle).

And it's not that God despised mankind, because they were still His children. It's just that He could not allow them to corrupt

---

14   *Who Was Noah's Wife?* Dr. Tim Chaffey (January 2015). Answers in Genesis.
      https://answersingenesis.org/bible-characters/noah/who-was-noahs-wife/

His plans for the future. A world filled with those that opposed His goodness would corrupt those plans, and they just could not be allowed to persist. This explains why God later commanded the Israelites to destroy the inhabitants of the cities they would occupy (read the OT book of Joshua), and why God put Ananias and Sapphira to death (Acts 5:1-11) during the Church's beginnings; yet not for their sin, but to prevent the spreading of corruption from within.

> *Then I saw a new heaven and a new earth; for the first heaven and the first earth passed away, and there is no longer any sea.*
> REVELATION 21:1 NIV

> *"For look, I am ready to create new heavens and a new earth! The former ones will not be remembered; no one will think about them anymore."*
> ISAIAH 65:17 NET

As in the days of Noah, the new earth described above will and must be absent of those who stand in opposition to God. **Since the new earth is intended for eternal fellowship with God, why should those who do not desire His fellowship be included?**

Instead, those who choose to live eternally separated from God shall be gathered together in the same place—where no goodness exists. For when you remove the impurities from an element, what can be done with those impurities? Don't they, by definition, contain no measured goodness? Must you not keep them separate from the now pure element? Or is there a method by which waste matter can be made good and reintroduced?

While a father might be forced to kick his rebellious son out into the streets—for the sake of the others in the household— there is typically always a hope for future reconciliation. But in this case, God was brokenhearted; not that He created them, but that they could not stay in His house. There could be no reconciliation.

> *So the* LORD *said, "My Spirit will not remain in humankind indefinitely, since they are mortal. They will remain for 120 more years."*
> GENESIS 6:3 NET

But God waiting for Noah and his boys and their wives to serve as the new Adam and Eve is an exciting and encouraging concept, as it can bring us a bit of resolution in regard to why some children are often permitted by God to be born into such terrible situations. We know that God allows the weeds to grow up alongside the good seed:

> *Jesus told them another parable: "The kingdom of heaven is like a man who sowed good seed in his field. But while everyone was sleeping, his enemy came and sowed weeds among the wheat, and went away. When the wheat sprouted and formed heads, then the weeds also appeared.*
> *The owner's servants came to him and said, 'Sir, didn't you sow good seed in your field? Where then did the weeds come from?'*
> *'An enemy did this,' he replied.*
> *The servants asked him, 'Do you want us to go and pull them up?'*
> *"'No,' he answered, 'because while you are pulling the weeds, you may uproot the wheat with them. Let both grow together until the harvest. At that time I will tell the harvesters: First collect the weeds and tie them in bundles to be burned; then gather the wheat and bring it into my barn.'"*
> MATTHEW 13:24-30 NIV

But He also knows the generations of parents required to bring forth the individuals through whom He intends to bring change.

We see this play out in virtually every major family recorded in the Old Testament. Dysfunctional family after dysfunctional family, we still see specific individuals "raised up" through the centuries being established as keyframes in the moving picture of Jewish history.

Abraham slept with his wife's servant (wait, what?); Isaac and Rebekah showed favoritism to each of their twin sons; Jacob (Israel) had thirteen children from four different women; and his ten eldest boys grew up and sold their younger brother into slavery, telling their father he'd been killed. And yet, years later when those brothers came to Egypt to buy grain amid a great famine:

> *He said, "I am your brother Joseph, the one you sold into Egypt! And now, do not be distressed and do not be angry with yourselves for selling me here, because it was to save lives that God sent me ahead of you."*
>
> GENESIS 45:4-5 NIV

All said and done, God judged all of mankind and had chosen Noah, long before he was born, to be the father (ancestor) of Abraham, who would become the father of many nations (Genesis 17:4-5, Romans 4:17-18). By submerging the earth in water, God performed a great purification by washing away the impurities found on the surface of the earth. Because God determined that all mankind—save Noah and his immediate family—was corrupt and "full of violence," the hundreds of millions of people alive at that time were sentenced to death.

Okay. So we know that Noah was five hundred years old when the oldest of his three boys were born, and the Flood came a hundred years later. And during those hundred years, all three boys grew up and found wives, and in that time God had given Noah the order and direction to begin construction on the ark. Again, it's possible (and very likely) that these younger couples each had their own kids during the time leading up to the Flood.

However, if they did, those kids would have long since moved away and become a part of the world in which they lived. For when the time of judgment came, only Noah and his immediate family, only eight in all, were saved from that judgment. And not only were they saved, but they became the instruments through whom God would redeem all that was lost.

> *Noah was 600 years old when the floodwaters engulfed the earth. Noah entered the ark along with his sons, his wife, and his sons' wives because of the floodwaters.*
> Genesis 7:6-7 NET

Now this was purification by immersion. The entire surface of the earth was engulfed by the floodwaters. While God's judgment was "poured out" on Noah's world and was the end for all those who perished, we must also understand that this purification—though accomplished by the water—was not performed by the water. Indeed, this purification occurred by the power of God, manifested through the Holy Spirit.

> *In the beginning God created the heavens and the earth. Now the earth was formless and empty, darkness was over the surface of the deep, and the Spirit of God was hovering over the waters.*
> Genesis 1:1-2 NIV

God provided the warning. God instructed Noah on the building of the ark. God summoned the animals to be saved and brought them to Noah for loading. God closed up and sealed the ark. God brought the floodwaters. And then God caused the floodwaters to withdraw when the time was right.

For it was God who was creating a new earth. And those who chose to reject God had made an everlasting decision they did not understand, just as those today do not understand the gravity of their decision to stand in their pride and die in their sin. As a result, only the eight of Noah's family—and all the animals on the ark—would be allowed admittance to the new earth.

Interestingly, these passages in Genesis give no indication that Noah ever spoke to anyone specifically about the flood, and there's nothing to suggest that Noah spent any of his time preaching. And since the whole world stood condemned, who exactly would he have preached to and what message would he have preached? There's no indication that he was a prophet (though ancient rabbinical texts suggest so), and God did not command him to "Tell the people . . ."

So, the traditional premise that the people of his day ridiculed and rejected Noah seems unfounded. In fact, there's no record of a single word spoken by Noah until he utters his curse upon his son Ham and his descendants (Canaan) in Genesis 9:24. Yet later generations still suggested such things, giving birth to tradition and myth. This was true in the Jewish culture (through which the Midrash and Talmud were born) and in Christianity—as we have already seen examples of thousands of writings from respected leaders in the early Church—as well as hundreds of thousands of books and commentaries (present company included) on the interpretations of Scripture.

> *You have seen a man wise in his own opinion–there is more hope for a fool than for him.*
> PROVERBS 26:12 NET

The New Has Come
Chapter 4: Rebirth and Renewal

In the six hundredth year of Noah's life, on the seventeenth day of the second month—on that day all the springs of the great deep burst forth, and the floodgates of the heavens were opened. And rain fell on the earth forty days and forty nights.

Genesis 7:11-12 NIV

WHETHER IT HAD RAINED ON THE EARTH before that day or not, the rain had to come from somewhere. The Bible says that water surged up from underground and fell from the sky, but we know that the rain would have had to accumulate from the waters below.

We know this, because that's how clouds and rain work. There couldn't have been a thick layer of cloud engulfing the entire planet since Creation—which would have kept the sun and moon from being seen—though just such a cloud cover would have had to be manufactured at some point before it started raining. So, it appears God released the waters from the deep, accelerated the process to form the clouds, and perpetuated that cycle over the entire surface of the earth for the next forty days.

And although the rain lasted only forty days and nights (it rained non-stop for well over a month), for five months the floodwaters continued to persist until all life "that had breath" had perished, except for life on the ark[15] and in the sea. Because the fresh rainwater would have floated separately on top of the seas, God may have employed more natural processes for this "new" water to evaporate back into the atmosphere, as well as allowing time for the new and existing vegetation to regrow.

In his first letter, the apostle Peter makes a connection between the Flood and baptism, but let's take a look at its context. Peter is discussing a larger topic regarding all Christians being an example to one another and their community at large. As Paul does in 1 Corinthians, so Peter is doing here, across his entire letter, instructing all disciples in right living and interaction with everyone.

At this particular point of his letter, Peter reminds his readers of Christ's assertion that "they will have trouble" (John 16:33, Mark 10:30), and that they should treat any persecution as "a blessing".

> *But even if you suffer for doing what is right, God will reward you for it. So don't worry or be afraid of their threats. Instead, you must worship Christ as Lord of your life. And if someone asks about your hope as a believer, always be ready to explain it. But do this in a gentle and respectful way. Keep your conscience clear. Then if people speak against you, they will be ashamed when they see what a good life you live because you belong to Christ. Remember, it is better to suffer for doing*

---

15   **aron** *(aw-rōn´)—Hebrew.* Normally translated as "ark". This Hebrew word can mean cabinet or box, but is always understood in the context or purpose of a vessel or vehicle. In the book of Exodus, God instructs Moses to manufacture the "ark of the covenant." Then "You shall put the mercy seat on top of the *[aron]*, and in the *[aron]* you shall put the testimony which I will give to you. There I will meet with you; and from above the mercy seat, from between the two cherubim which are upon the *[aron]* of the testimony, I will speak to you about all that I will give you in commandment for the sons of Israel (Exodus 25:21-22 NIV)." The ark of the covenant, or ark of the testimony, which was much more than just a container or a box, was literally a sacred place where the presence of God could reside with the Israelites. This tells us that the floating container that Noah built should be seen more as a temple or sanctuary than a boat. And, more appropriately, it represented a dwelling place of God.

good, if that is what God wants, than to suffer for doing wrong!
1 PETER 3:14-17 NLT

Then, Peter gives an example of the days of Noah and how they correspond to the present.

For Christ also suffered for sins once for all time, the just for the unjust, so that He might bring us to God, having been put to death in the flesh, but made alive in the spirit; in which He also went and made proclamation to the spirits in prison, who once were disobedient when the patience of God kept waiting in the days of Noah, during the construction of the ark, in which a few, that is, eight persons, were brought safely through the water.
1 PETER 3:18-20 NASB

Those in Noah's day rebelled against God, obviously. And Peter seems to be using Noah as an example of persecution and of those who spoke against him. However, as noted previously, there's nothing in the text of Genesis to suggest any significant interaction between Noah and the people in the area where he lived (there's no record of him speaking to anyone prior to the flood).

"As it was in the days of Noah, so it will be at the coming of the Son of Man. For in the days before the flood, people were eating and drinking, marrying and giving in marriage, up to the day Noah entered the ark; and they knew nothing about what would happen until the flood came and took them all away. That is how it will be at the coming of the Son of Man."
MATTHEW 24:37-39 NIV

Of course, common sense would suggest that over the course of 600 years, Noah interacted with many people. And when the day came to start building the ark, it's quite reasonable to assume that his neighbors had something to say about it. Since Peter is writing inspired words, it's also reasonable to assume that he has been given special revelation or insight as to those historic events.

Additionally, rabbinical teaching had already added some mythical components to this story years before Peter was born, and it's very likely that these things had influenced all Jewish thought by that time. Remember, Jewish traditions and man-made ideas had been formed long before Jesus walked the earth.

But we must not interpret these things that seem out-of-place and off-topic as being so. Peter is making a larger point here, and this reference to Noah and the Flood are part of that point. He is not introducing a separate teaching in the middle of another.

Peter declares that "it is better to suffer for doing good," and then reminds us that "Christ also suffered," having been put to death but "made alive in the spirit." Now, in the Spirit, Jesus is not confined to time and space, but can then go and speak to those who have died prior to His resurrection. Not just those who perished in the Flood, but every soul since then who awaits the Day of Judgment. Peter repeats this same sentiment in his very next paragraph:

> *But they will have to give account to him who is ready to judge the living and the dead. For this is the reason the gospel was preached even to those who are now dead, so that they might be judged according to human standards in regard to the body, but live according to God in regard to the spirit.*
>
> 1 Peter 4:5-6 NIV

An early Church leader, Augustine of Hippo (354-430 AD), understood that what Peter is doing is declaring that Jesus, as the Holy Spirit, had gone "and made proclamation" through Noah, who spoke in the power of the Spirit of Christ, to all those souls of his day who ultimately rejected the need to "repent, for the kingdom of heaven" was near (Matthew 3:2 NET). Augustine writes:

> For that transaction had been typical of future events, so that those who do not believe the gospel in our age, when the Church is being built up in all nations, may be understood to be like those who did not believe in that age while the ark was a preparing . . .
>
> But to the men of Noah's time the gospel was preached in vain, because they believed not when God's long suffering waited for them during the many years in which the ark was being built (for the building of the ark was itself in a certain sense a preaching of mercy); even as now men similar to them are unbelieving, who, to use the same figure, are shut up in the darkness of ignorance as in a prison, beholding in vain the Church which is being built up throughout the world, while judgment is impending, as the flood was by which at that time all the unbelieving perished . . .
> —*Augustine, Epistle 164, Chapter 5* [16]

Did Noah and his family suffer persecution for obeying God? Maybe. Genesis doesn't tell us so, but Peter suggests it by referencing Noah here in the context of suffering. He also states in his second letter that "Noah warned the world of God's righteous judgment" (2 Peter 2:5 NLT).

But Peter's main reason for mentioning the Flood is that, just as only a small remnant (eight) were saved through the floodwaters then, God has saved us also. He has plucked us out of the corruption of the world and saved us—by electing to send His Son to die on a cross instead—as He waits patiently, "not wanting anyone to perish, but everyone to come to repentance" (2 Peter 3:9). This is important, as Peter wants us to understand that we have already been saved, and that the corruption of the world has no hold on us.

Did the waters of the Flood save Noah? Certainly not. God

---

16 *Augustine Letter 164 to Evodius on the subject of 1 Peter 3:21.*
   https://www.newadvent.org/fathers/1102164.htm

gave Noah and his family a choice, and they chose well. They were obedient to God, built the ark and got into it, so that by God's grace (as He'd already deemed them "righteous") they were rescued from the water. Yet it was that very water that was poured out onto the earth to purify it, so that Noah and his family could be ultimately saved by God with the water—that washed away the impurities of the world—as the ark was lifted high above the raging sea by the sea itself. And as a result, those eight were eventually able to step out into a new creation, and live new lives.

It is from this truth that we look again at Peter's words:

> *And that water is a picture of baptism, which now saves you, not by removing dirt from your body, but as a response to God from a clean conscience. It is effective because of the resurrection of Jesus Christ.*
> 1 PETER 3:21-22 NLT

A response. A clean conscience. An acceptance of God's mercy and grace that Jesus died for the sins of the world so that "because of the resurrection of Jesus Christ" we may be saved. Remember, if Jesus never rose from the dead, we would have no hope . . . for anything. Peter reminds us of this in his introduction, and it serves as the theme of his entire letter:

> *Praise be to the God and Father of our Lord Jesus Christ! In his great mercy he has given us new birth into a living hope through the resurrection of Jesus Christ from the dead, and into an inheritance that can never perish, spoil or fade.*
> 1 PETER 1:3-4 NIV

Having accepted Jesus' sacrifice, we logically respond to God through our repentance and obedience. Not an obedience born from a place of fear, but from one of love, gratitude and respect. For it is by our faith that we have accepted Christ, and by that faith we open our lives to transformation. And it is by that faith that we are saved:

> *And without faith it is impossible to please God, because anyone who comes to him must believe that he exists and that he rewards those who earnestly seek him. By faith Noah, when warned about things not yet seen, in holy fear built an ark to save his family. By his faith he condemned the world and became heir of the righteousness that is in keeping with faith.*
> Hebrews 11:6-7 NIV

It is this obedience of faith that Peter speaks of when relating to baptism. So while the water itself does not save, there is clearly an expectation that all members of his audience had indeed been baptized. Paul had this same understanding (since he had personally baptized many) as he addressed the recipients in his letter to the Christians in Rome:

> *How shall we who died to sin still live in it? Or do you not know that all of us who have been baptized into Christ Jesus have been baptized into His death? Therefore we have been buried with Him through baptism into death, so that as Christ was raised from the dead through the glory of the Father, so we too might walk in newness of life.*
> Romans 6:2-4 NASB

> *For all of you who were baptized into Christ have clothed yourselves with Christ.*
> Galatians 3:27 NIV

> *For you were buried with Christ when you were baptized. And with him you were raised to new life because you trusted the mighty power of God, who raised Christ from the dead.*
> Colossians 2:12 NLT

Through it all, we can see that there was an historical understanding and connection between the Flood and Christian baptism. In the chapters ahead, we'll continue to investigate the hows and the whys. But from here we can clearly see that the Flood was foundational to everything, as it represented a new earth and a new creation.

> *This means that anyone who belongs to Christ has become a new person. The old life is gone; a new life has begun!*
>
> 2 Corinthians 5:17 NLT

Is It Just Me or Is It Hot in Here?
Chapter 5: The Dead Zone

Now, as we've tried to give clarity to Peter's comments regarding the Flood, there's another school of fish, er, thought, regarding Jesus' descent into hell. We've read this before:

> *For this reason the gospel was preached also to those who are dead, that they might be judged according to men in the flesh, but live according to God in the spirit.*
>
> 1 Peter 4:6 NKJV

Does this say Jesus went to hell to preach to the dead? Or might it instead refer to all who have heard the gospel in their lifetime who are now dead?

Until now, I've really argued against Christ's descension in this context because it's not mentioned in the gospels. There are a couple of ambiguous passages authored by the apostles Peter and Paul that the Catholic Church uses as a basis for this teaching, though they aren't clear enough to convince us on their own.

> *Therefore He says: "When He ascended on high, He led captivity captive, and gave gifts to men." (Now this, "He ascended"–what does it mean but that He also first descended into the lower parts of the earth? He who descended is also the One who*

> *ascended far above all the heavens, that He might fill all things.)*
> Ephesians 4:8-10 NKJV

In this text, can it be assumed that the "lower parts of the earth" means "hell"? It could, but if Paul meant "hell", why didn't he just use the terms that everyone already understood? *Gehenna* was a very common term in Judaism. So how can one make the leap that *lower parts of the earth* could really mean that eternal place of torment, since hell is not located underground, and nobody believed it was.

The Greek text of this passage uses the term *katōteros gē meros*, which could just as plainly be translated as "the lower earthly region." More clearly, we hear this from Jesus Himself:

> *"No one has ascended into heaven except the one who descended from heaven–the Son of Man."*
> John 3:13 NASB

Interestingly, the *Apostle's Creed* does state specifically that Jesus "descended into hell" (added at the Council of Florence in 1445). But you may not know that the Apostle's Creed is a revision of the earlier *Nicene Creed*, adopted officially in 381 AD, which *does not* make this claim. But the Catholic Church makes their understanding and teaching of this doctrine clear:

> The frequent New Testament affirmations that Jesus was "raised from the dead" presuppose that the crucified one sojourned in the realm of the dead prior to his resurrection. This was the first meaning given in the apostolic preaching to Christ's descent into hell: that Jesus, like all men, experienced death and in his soul joined the others in the realm of the dead. But he descended there as Saviour, proclaiming the Good News to the spirits imprisoned there.
> Scripture calls the abode of the dead, to which the dead Christ went down, "hell"—Sheol in Hebrew or Hades in

Greek—because those who are there are deprived of the vision of God. Such is the case for all the dead, *whether evil or righteous*, while they await the Redeemer: which does not mean that their lot is identical, as Jesus shows through the parable of the poor man Lazarus who was received into "Abraham's bosom."

It is precisely these holy souls, who awaited their Savior in Abraham's bosom, whom Christ the Lord delivered when he descended into hell. Jesus did not descend into hell to deliver the damned, nor to destroy the hell of damnation, but to free the just who had gone before him.
—*Catechism of the Catholic Church, 632-633* [17]

Originally, I was going to suggest that Jesus had been clear that those who are in hell cannot return from the abyss, regardless of any after-the-fact preaching, by Himself or anyone else, as He explains in His parable of the rich man and Lazarus. It's referenced above, but let's read it in fuller context:

> "The time came when the beggar died and the angels carried [Lazarus] to Abraham's side. The rich man also died and was buried. In Hades, where he was in torment, he looked up and saw Abraham far away, with Lazarus by his side. So he called to him, 'Father Abraham, have pity on me and send Lazarus to dip the tip of his finger in water and cool my tongue, because I am in agony in this fire.'
>
> "But Abraham replied, 'Son, remember that in your lifetime you received your good things, while Lazarus received bad things, but now he is comforted here and you are in agony. And besides all this, between us and you a great chasm has been set in place, so that those who want to go from here to you cannot, nor can anyone cross over from there to us.'"
>
> LUKE 16:22-26 NIV

---

17   *Catechism of the Catholic Church.* https://www.vatican.va/archive/ENG0015/__P2N.HTM

Until I read the Catholic Church's *catechism* quoted above, I really didn't agree with the idea of Christ going to hell (for I understood this to be the hell of final judgment, *Gehenna* or *Hades*) to preach to those already lost. I'd even confused this idea with the meaning of the passage from 1 Peter at the beginning of this chapter.

But now, after having read the Catholic Church's understanding of this part of the Creed, it actually brings clarity and resolution. "Hell" in this latter context is not the hell of eternity, but rather the timeless place of rest (*Sheol*) between the body's death and the Day of Reckoning. As the catechism states, and the gospel of John attests, Jesus was definitely "raised from the dead."

As I've noted elsewhere, Jewish law prescribed that one must be dead for three full days to be declared legally dead. That's why Jesus waited to raise Lazarus until the fourth day, and why Jesus remained in the ground for three full days. Any premature resurrections wouldn't have counted as legitimate.

Prior to all this, I kind of believed that all who die (and have ever died) are immediately removed from the timeline and brought before Christ for judgment. In this way, since there is no time, the dead don't have to wait around, but instantly find themselves in the presence of the Lord on Judgment Day. This idea makes sense of us speaking of deceased loved-ones as being "in a better place", "going home," or going "to be with God."

But now, what this new understanding means to me is that there is most certainly a place between death and Final Judgment.

I'd recently read Lee Strobel's book *The Case for Heaven,*[18] and I was struck by the truth of this. In it, the author noted a number of folks who each had an out-of-body or near-death experience (NDE). Each experience was recorded by an individual who was clinically dead, and yet returned to the place of the living, later recounting details of their experiences during death. In some

---

18   *The Case for Heaven: A Journalist Investigates Evidence for Life After Death.* Lee Strobel (Zondervan, 2021)

cases, patients were dead on arrival, and yet were able to provide verifiable details about staff, objects, and conversations they would not have been privy to while on the operating table.

Anyway, my point is that I must agree with the Catholic teaching on this point. While there are no more resurrections in this age, there are certainly regular occurrences of people experiencing clinical death, some who are revived with great effort on the part of medical personnel, some in comas, and many who lie in hospital beds indefinitely with machines working to keep their bodies from reaching the point of no return. With this the case, there must be a "dead zone" where temporary existence occurs.

It is this very non-physical place that Jesus must also have been a resident of for the thirty-six hours following His last breath on the cross that Wednesday afternoon.

This implies that when Jesus died, everyone else who had died prior to that had already been hanging out in that dead zone too. Of course, I still suspect there is no measure of time there, and that these souls would experience a rather *instantaneous* movement from death to eternity when that Day comes. From those since Noah's day until Jesus' day, each and all would experience having "just arrived" at the same time, even though it hasn't yet happened from our perspective.

So, while the outside world waited three days, Jesus had all the time in the world.

For Star Trek fans, this idea was cleverly, though perhaps unintentionally, represented in the film *Star Trek: Generations*.[19] In what would become James T. Kirk's final chapter, Kirk has been trapped in a galactic energy ribbon called the "Nexus" as a result of an event that left him presumed dead many years earlier. But when the captain of the next generation of the *USS Enterprise*, Jean-Luc Picard, shows up in that same Nexus seventy years later, Kirk explains to Picard how it seemed he'd only "just arrived."

Now, you don't have to agree with the idea of timelessness in

---

19   *Star Trek Generations.* Paramount Pictures (1994)

the dead zone, but there's really no arguing the existence of that in-between space between life and the everlasting.

POSTPONING PURGATORY

Regardless of how one may interpret this dead zone before final judgment, this concept may have given rise to the theological idea of a purgatory (Latin, *purgare*, a place of purging or purification), a temporary place where many saints (allegedly) get to hang out (against their will) indefinitely before entering the glory of heaven. Now this idea of an expiatory holding tank, wherein one would remain until their purification was complete, plainly contradicts Jesus' atoning work on the cross and the purification that is performed through the work of the Holy Spirit Himself—something not accomplished by the additional work of our own efforts! For if Jesus has already made the atonement for our sins (once for all, right?), and the Holy Spirit is doing all the work of our purification, why must He wait until after we die to finish the work (again)?

> *. . . while we wait for the blessed hope–the appearing of the glory of our great God and Savior, Jesus Christ, who gave himself for us to redeem us from all wickedness and to purify for himself a people that are his very own, eager to do what is good.*
> Titus 2:13-14 NIV

> *By his will we have been made holy through the offering of the body of Jesus Christ once for all . . . For by one offering he has perfected for all time those who are made holy.*
> Hebrews 10:10, 14 NET

He himself is the sacrifice that atones for our sins—and not only our sins but the sins of all the world.

1 JOHN 2:2 NLT

For God was in Christ, reconciling the world to himself, no longer counting people's sins against them.

2 CORINTHIANS 5:19 NLT

The next day [John] saw Jesus coming to him and said, "Behold, the Lamb of God who takes away the sin of the world!"

JOHN 1:29 NASB

Remarkably, this concept of purgatory doesn't seem to have even come into Roman Catholic doctrine until late in the thirteenth century. It's understood that, at the Second Council of Lyon in 1274 (and later ratified at the Council of Florence in 1431—and there may be a test later on this stuff, so pay attention), this doctrine was first defined to impress two specific points that had been invented: 1) that "some souls are purified after death," and 2) that "such souls benefit from the prayers and pious duties that the living do for them." These duties, such as prayers and alms (contributions), are intended to relieve the distress of those in purgatory undergoing final refinement.

But what refinement could actually be occurring and by whom is it being performed?

While this doctrine finds its origins in the Jewish practice of "praying for the dead" (2 Maccabees 12:42-45, *apocryphal*), which permeated Church culture for centuries, there seems to be no historical record of purgatory being suggested until such time as the Church felt they needed to work it out in the aforementioned council. There is no other scriptural support for it, and no examples or discussions of its practice are found in any letters or documents penned by any of the early Church fathers.[20]

Even still, Catholic "evidence" for this idea is given primarily via 1 Corinthians 3:10-15, where there's an indication that "fire" will test the quality of one's life. Taken out of context, this passage could indicate that some (if not most) Christians who were less virtuous would require additional refinement (apparently because the Holy Spirit was incompetent) before their allowance into heaven.

But using this logic, how could anyone know who got the non-stop flight and who got laid over? Since purgatory, by definition, is a place for only those who are already saved (if even by the skin of their teeth), then there's really no concern for their salvation. The concern (and by extension offerings and prayers) is only in regard to their endurance through the "fires of refinement" and not of the agonizing torture they would otherwise experience in the flames of the eternal hell.

Since the idea of purgatory is intentionally tied to giving alms and prayers for the dead (so that parishioners might increase their contributions, I suppose), wouldn't it be logical to assume that *everyone* goes to purgatory? I mean, how can any of us be sure someone was ever virtuous enough to go straight to heaven? Shouldn't we simply assume that nobody is righteous enough, and everyone will require some final refinement?

So let's take a look to see what Scripture says.

The apostle Paul is writing, in 1 Corinthians 3, about concerns in the Corinthian church, as some members were claiming to be either "disciples" of Paul himself or followers of other leaders who had baptized them, such as Apollos or the apostle Peter (Cephas).

---

20   Interestingly, the term "church father" is erroneous. These men were simply leaders in the early Church who wrote stuff down or otherwise had an opinion about something. None of them had been apostles, and very few of them had a direct connection to any of the apostles. The apostolic Church had been established long before any of these other men came into being, and therefore are in no way fathers of the Church. Only the original apostles could rightfully hold that designation, in the same way that Abraham, Isaac and Jacob are considered the fathers of the nation of Israel.

Here, the satan[21] was already sowing the seeds of division in the Church from early on. This issue was akin to the modern-day reality of churchgoers leaving a particular congregation because their favorite pastor had moved or resigned. But Paul explains to his readers that all church leaders are servants of Christ and are simply humans who have been *appointed* by God to serve the kingdom of God.

> *Because of God's grace to me, I have laid the foundation like an expert builder. Now others are building on it. But whoever is building on this foundation must be very careful. For no one can lay any foundation other than the one we already have—Jesus Christ.*
>
> *Anyone who builds on that foundation may use a variety of materials—gold, silver, jewels, wood, hay, or straw. But on the judgment day, fire will reveal what kind of work each builder has done. The fire will show if a person's work has any value. If the work survives, that builder will receive a reward. But if the work is burned up, the builder will suffer great loss. The builder will be saved, but like someone barely escaping through a wall of flames.*
>
> 1 Corinthians 3:10-15 NLT

And keep in mind that this letter was not originally penned in chapters and verses, it was just one big letter. And the thought Paul covers in chapter three actually begins in the middle of chapter two, which then carries all the way through to the end of chapter four. In this larger context, we find that Paul isn't speaking at all about our "works" or deeds here on earth, or whether we are "righteous" enough to enter heaven directly.

Instead, we can plainly see that he's referring specifically to some apparent false teachers who had otherwise come into their congregation and were trying to convince the people of things

---

21   *Who is Satan?* by John Gregory Drummond (January 2023). Biblical Archaeology Society. https://www.biblicalarchaeology.org/daily/biblical-topics/bible-interpretation/who-is-satan/

contrary to what Paul, Peter or Apollos had preached to them regarding their own salvation. And, most importantly, that as disciples of Christ, they (and we) should all be following Jesus instead of being wrapped up in who the next great "man of God" is.

His last words in that passage state, "But if the work is burned up, the builder will suffer great loss. The builder will be saved, but like someone barely escaping through a wall of flames." This conjures up the image of one escaping a burning building (that he alone had inadvertently set ablaze), who manages to heave himself out the front door in the nick of time as the building collapses around him. For him, there is no reward since he is to blame for the fire, though he escapes with his life and the smoldering shirt on his back.

For it is the works—and more specifically the teachings—of those who lead or teach the body of Christ (in any way, shape or form) that will be "tested" by fire, and not the individuals themselves. Paul says that it is *their work* that will be shown for what it is. If they are building on the foundation of the gospel using strong, valuable teaching (gold, silver, precious gems), then they will be rewarded by Jesus on the Last Day. But if they use poor, unbiblical teaching (wood, hay, straw), then they will "suffer great loss" because all they have "built up" will be burned up. Paul's words here are not applicable to every Christian who walks with Jesus, but to any and all who serve as leaders and to those who offer instruction to other believers.

The exception, obviously, is the one who teaches false doctrine intentionally, with the purpose of advancing his own personal agenda or glorification.[22]

> *But false prophets arose among the people, just as there will*
> *be false teachers among you. These false teachers will infiltrate*
> *your midst with destructive heresies, even to the point of*
> *denying the Master who bought them. As a result, they will*

---

22   *What Makes a False Teacher?* by Zachary Wagner, Center for Pastor Theologians (August 2021). https://www.pastortheologians.com/articles/2021/8/13/what-makes-a-false-teacher-false

> *bring swift destruction on themselves. And many will follow their debauched lifestyles. Because of these false teachers, the way of truth will be slandered. And in their greed they will exploit you with deceptive words.*

2 Peter 1-3 NET

We'll look more closely at the concept of purification and atonement later, but for now, let's get our eyes on what circumcision is all about, being careful not to touch anything.

Cutting to the Quick

Chapter 6: Circumspect Circumstances

*Eight days later, when the baby was circumcised, he was
named Jesus, the name given him by the angel even before
he was conceived.*

Luke 2:21 NLT

Jewish law was clear on this subject. On the eighth day
following a boy's birth, he was to be presented to the priests
and circumcised. From turtle to fireman, he would undergo a
transformation he would never remember because of a promise
that would never be forgotten. But why? What was this all about?
Where did this law come from?

The Law of Moses (Hebrew *Torah*, Greek *Pentateuch*)
represents the first five books of the Hebrew Bible: Genesis,
Exodus, Leviticus, Numbers and Deuteronomy. These books are
believed to have been first put into writing by Moses[23] during the
Israelites' time in the wilderness following the Exodus (which
you can read all about in the Old Testament book of the same
name).

Since it would have taken years for Moses to finish getting it
all down onto parchment and collected into scrolls, everything
had to first be communicated verbally, or orally. God gave His
Word to Moses and Aaron, who in turn gave it to the elders,
who in turn gave it to the clan and tribal leaders, who in turn

---

23   *Patterns of Evidence: The Moses Controversy.* Thinking Man Films (2019)

gave it to the heads of each household, who then gave it to their families and servants. This was the process and foundation of the oral tradition. By the time Moses had put in writing all of God's commands, the Israelites had long since been putting them all into practice.

But the history of the Hebrew nation was being born during that time, and nobody really thought much about their heritage. Though they were fully aware of that heritage and knew to which tribe they belonged (we see this clarified in the census taken in the first chapter of Numbers), the Israelites alive at that time had considered themselves as having always been slaves in Egypt (since those alive had always been), and so their identity had been kind of lost. This is reflected in the way the Israelites saw themselves:

> *Then [the Israelites] said to Moses, "Is it because there were no graves in Egypt that you have taken us away to die in the wilderness? Why have you dealt with us in this way, bringing us out of Egypt? ... For it would have been better for us to serve the Egyptians than to die in the wilderness."*
> EXODUS 14:11-12 NASB

> *The Israelites said to [Moses and Aaron], "If only we had died by the hand of the LORD in the land of Egypt, when we sat by the pots of meat, when we ate bread to the full, for you have brought us out into this wilderness to kill this whole assembly with hunger!"*
> EXODUS 16:3 NET

The primary purpose of Genesis was not to tell the rest of the world where the Jewish people came from, but to help the children of God understand where *they* came from. Through that telling, they would come to see how God had chosen them long before they were born to be His special possession. Isn't this the purpose of the Scriptures for Christians too?

Just as today, we pretend not to give too much thought about where we come from, even though we spend millions of dollars each year searching family trees or chasing down our birth parents once we learn we've been adopted. Ironically, we learn and know very little of our history as a nation, and oftentimes there are forces at work to change or erase that history.

But all the while, we're still greatly concerned about where we're going and how we're going to get there. *What's the quickest and most painless way? Give me the shortcuts! Don't explain it to me, just show me!* As we race through this world of instant gratification, it's hard to imagine what it must have been like for the Israelites to have wandered through that Middle Eastern desert for forty years and wait upon the LORD.

But at the mountain of Sinai, just a relatively short while after the Israelites' adventure through the Red Sea, God summoned Moses to the top of that mountain (this was the same place where God had first appeared to Moses from the burning bush) and gave him loads of direction and commands on how to lead the people to the land God had promised their ancestors—to a land that would most certainly be "flowing with milk and honey."

Through those Ten Commandments and a variety of other detailed instructions, God spoke through Moses to the Israelite multitude to begin building a nation that was to be set apart as God's chosen people.[24] But before God could build them up, He needed to prepare them. He had to move them into a position where they could receive what He would give them—a mental, physical, and spiritual position that would allow Him to work in their hearts to accomplish His plan.

So God moved the Israelites into a position of isolation, into

---

24   **qadas** (*kaw-dosh´*)—*Hebrew.* Holy, holiness, sacred, set apart. Holiness is a conferred status. It is not something that can be pursued and achieved. God is holy and He conferred that holy status on Israel so that He could remain living among them. God's presence brought benefit and relationship, but Israel's failure to take their status into account when considering their behavior brought consequences. That status could not be gained or lost, but God's presence could be. In the same way, the body of Christ is considered a "holy nation" (1 Peter 2:9), a status to be neither gained nor lost, but one that must be considered when determining our behavior in heart, mind, soul and strength.

the wilderness so that they could be separated from the world around them, just as Noah and his family were separated from the world through the ark. For only in that new and unfamiliar place would they be in the "right place" to receive Him. **How much easier is it to receive the Word of God when we are in isolation?**

> *During the high-priesthood of Annas and Caiaphas, the word of God came to John son of Zechariah in the wilderness. He went into all the country around the Jordan, preaching a baptism of repentance for the forgiveness of sins.*
>
> Luke 3:2-3 NIV

> *Jesus, full of the Holy Spirit, left the Jordan and was led by the Spirit into the wilderness.*
>
> Luke 4:1 NIV

> *One day Moses was tending the flock of his father-in-law, Jethro, the priest of Midian. He led the flock far into the wilderness and came to Sinai, the mountain of God. There the angel of the LORD appeared to him in a blazing fire from the middle of a bush.*
>
> Exodus 3:1-2 NLT

Now the way that the Israelites would be set apart from the world around them—to demonstrate to the world that their God was the one true god—was to live differently, eat differently, love differently, and live out the uniqueness of being special in God's eyes. But to accomplish this, it would demand some serious rules and guidelines, and it would demand that such laws be followed to the letter. Sadly, the Israelites were never particularly obedient, and it begs to wonder, as the comedian/actor John Cleese of Monty Python fame puts it, why God didn't just "change his mind and pick a more cooperative bunch?"[25]

This came at a time when the rest of the world was already engaged in animal and human sacrifices. The surrounding nations were already engaged in polygamy, incest, and homosexuality. There was drunkenness, murder, and rape. There was slavery and human trafficking. People were thieves, they were greedy, and they coveted what others had. And for the many who were lacking, their envy would bring destruction to what others did have.

But God wanted His special children to be different from all of that. As He did with Noah over seven hundred years earlier, He was going to build a new ark, and He was going to save the world through the lives of the few. God intended to reconcile the entire world through the Jewish people, but He needed to prepare them for the task.

Instead of a boat, however, this ark was going to be the continuing promise God made with Abraham four hundred and thirty years before (Exodus 12:40). That promise, or covenant, was of the blessing that would result in Abraham becoming the "father of many nations." The Israelites didn't yet fully understand that God always keeps His promises, but their ancestor Abraham had come to learn that truth firsthand, which is why he had come to trust everything that God said, even when it sounded ludicrous.

NOT THE FIRST PROMISE

God had been making (and keeping) promises since the beginning of time. It started in Eden, if you'll recall, when He said:

> *"You may freely eat the fruit of every tree in the garden—except the tree of the knowledge of good and evil. If you eat its fruit,*

---

25   *So Anyway . . .* John Cleese (Crown Publishing, 2014)

> *you are sure to die."*
> GENESIS 2:16-17 NLT

Adam and Eve ate from it, were expelled from the Garden, and (albeit a thousand years later) died. They died because they no longer had access to the Tree of Life. In the days of Noah, God promised to make it rain for forty days and nights and destroy all life on the ground. And He did. After the Flood, God promised that He would never again send a flood to destroy the earth. And, well . . . so far, so good.

But when we go back those four hundred and thirty-plus years before the Exodus and read through Abraham's story (he was originally called Abram), we see him acting in faith towards God in obedience time and time again. Abram remained faithful from the moment he left his native country, his relatives, and his father's family, to the land that God would show him (Genesis 12:1), to the day he believed God would give him a son, even though he was already eighty-five and his wife (Sarai) was seventy-five and had been unable to have kids.

And so, one day, in a vision, God told Abram that he would have descendants as numerous as the stars in the sky. And because "Abram believed the LORD," God declared Abram as "righteous" (Genesis 15:6).

"Great!" thinks Abram. So he runs to his wife Sarai out in the garden and tells her the good news.

"Sweetheart! I just spoke with God. He says we're going to have a son!" Abram exclaims.

Sarai looks at him quizzically and says, "You know that I can't have children, right?"

"Oh. Yeah, I forgot about that," replies Abram, and he stares down at his feet.

"I have an idea," Sarai says. "Why don't you sleep with my servant girl, and then we'll have a son through her! If God says we're gonna have a son, then doggonit, we're gonna have a son!"

"Great idea!" Abram says. "I knew there was a reason I married you," and she leads him by the hand as they dash off toward her servant's tent.

They step into the young girl's tent to find her sewing what looks like men's pants.

"Hey, Hagar! Guess what? *We're going to have a baby!*"

Obviously, Sarai didn't really have a garden, but that's not the point. What's happening here is that Sarai had not yet experienced God's faithfulness in her own life; she didn't know God as Abram did.

Desperately wanting a child to mother, she hatched her own plan to have one. This wasn't God's plan, it was hers. And the result of that surrogacy played out as it often does today: the real mother decided to keep the baby.[26] Hagar became very proud and arrogant toward Sarai (*I can make babies and you can't!*), and it made things very weird.

How are you supposed to treat the mother of "your" child? Sarai wondered.

While Hagar contended with, *How do you treat an old woman who gave her husband permission to sleep with you? And how do you treat an old man who only slept with you so that he could have an heir, and has no love for you at all?*

And Abram's predicament, *What do you do with two wives who hate each other? Can't they just get along?*

Come along, Eliezer. Let's go hunting!

---

26   The solution proposed by Sarai is not as shocking or outlandish as it would seem to us today. In the ancient world, barrenness was a catastrophe because one of the primary roles of the family was to produce the next generation. The survival of the family line was of the highest value, and it depended on producing progeny. Whatever threat a second wife might pose to harmony in the family paled in comparison to the necessity of an heir being produced. This attempted remedy is consistent with contemporary practice as a strategy for heirship. This option was often more attractive than others because if the wife were divorced, there would be an economic impact on the family (she would take her dowry with her). Concubines bring no dowry, only their fertility, to the family. (Taken from the NIV Cultural Backgrounds Study Bible. Copyright © 2016 by Zondervan.)

Like I said . . . It got weird.

Sarai despised Hagar and her son Ishmael because of what they represented. The boy wasn't hers, and he was just a continuing reminder of what she didn't have . . . and couldn't have. God had promised Abram that he was going to have an heir, but that didn't necessarily include Sarai at all, did it? Even though Ishmael was legally hers, he wasn't *really* hers. And while Hagar was only a slave wife, birthing an heir gave her greater status socially.

Of course, as God does, He works with what He's got (Romans 8:28), and so God blesses Hagar and Ishmael, telling her that He "will increase [her] descendants so much that they will be too numerous to count" (Genesis 16:10). And so Abram's son, Ishmael, grew to be a fine, strapping young man—and for the next fourteen years he tried his best to earn his father's approval and learn his father's ways so that, when he was older, he could take over the family business.

But then one day, when Abram was ninety-nine years old, God appeared to him and made a firm promise. Not the casual and vague promise that "your family line will live on for millennia," but a real deal, sealed with *a sign*.

> *"This is my covenant with you: I will make you the father of a multitude of nations! What's more, I am changing your name. It will no longer be Abram. Instead, you will be called Abraham, for you will be the father of many nations. I will make you extremely fruitful. Your descendants will become many nations, and kings will be among them!"*
>
> GENESIS 17:4-6 NLT

God had chosen Abraham to be the funnel through whom the rest of His plan would flow. God's promise was invisible, though Abraham knew it was real. However, God demanded a quid pro quo. He was going to bless Abraham forever, but Abraham had to "sign" the agreement in blood. And because this was a wee bit bigger than a pinky-promise (we assume, though size wasn't important), something a bit more substantial would be required.

So God continues in verses 9-14:

> *"Your responsibility is to obey the terms of the covenant. You and all your descendants have this continual responsibility. This is the covenant that you and your descendants must keep: Each male among you must be circumcised. You must cut off the flesh of your foreskin as a sign of the covenant between me and you. From generation to generation, every male child must be circumcised on the eighth day after his birth.*
>
> *"This applies not only to members of your family but also to the servants born in your household and the foreign-born servants whom you have purchased. All must be circumcised. Your bodies will bear the mark of my everlasting covenant. Any male who fails to be circumcised will be cut off[27] from the covenant family for breaking the covenant."*
>
> GENESIS 17:9-14 NLT

I'm sorry, I clearly misunderstood you. It sounded like you said "circumcise."

So there it was, just hanging out there in the heat of the day.

Interestingly enough, God didn't invent circumcision that afternoon. It was a practice that had been going on for quite a while in a variety of other "civilized" cultures at the time.

In each of those instances, circumcision involved one of four basic themes: fertility, virility, maturity and genealogy—and, in every circumstance, circumcision was a rite of passage. As such, it was typically performed in adolescence, and it gave new identity to the one circumcised, incorporating him into a particular group. But in this moment, the way God was commanding it to be done seems to be unique among all others who practiced it.

But why were women excluded from this "mark" of the covenant? Well, while there is actually a thing called female

---

27   *No pun intended.*

circumcision (which I really don't care to talk about), the *NIV Cultural Backgrounds Study Bible* gives us this insight:[28]

> In light of today's concerns with gender issues, some have wondered why the sign of the covenant should be something that marks only males. Two cultural issues may offer an explanation: patrilineal descent and identity in the community.
>
> (1) The concept of patrilineal descent resulted in males being considered the representatives of the clan and the ones through whom clan identity was preserved (as, e.g., the wife took on the tribal and clan identity of her husband).
>
> (2) Individuals found their identity more in the clan and the community than in a concept of self. Decisions and commitments were made by the family and clan more than by the individual.
>
> The rite of passage represented in circumcision marked each male as entering a clan committed to the covenant, a commitment that he would then have the responsibility to maintain. If this logic holds, circumcision would not focus on individual participation in the covenant as much as on continuing communal participation. The community is structured around patrilineal descent, so the sign on the males marks the corporate commitment of the clan from generation to generation.

Understanding this, it may be reasonable to see the correlation between circumcision and baptism, and perhaps the value of a greater connection to the community through baptism, not just as an act by an individual. Something to consider at least.

Before we continue, it's extremely important to note that what follows this instruction of circumcision (in verse 15) is God's affirmation of His covenant with Abram through his offspring.

---

28   *NIV Cultural Backgrounds Study Bible,* with notes from Dr. John H. Walton (Wheaton College) in the Old Testament and Dr. Craig S. Keener (Asbury Theological Seminary) in the New Testament. Copyright © 2016 by Zondervan.

At this point, God changes Abram's name to Abraham, and Sarai's to Sarah, declaring that they will both be the parents of many nations, and that one day soon Sarah would give birth to her own baby boy whom they would name Isaac. **Moreover, the promise God made to them at this time was given *before* Abraham actually circumcised anybody.**

A PART OF THE FAMILY

Understanding the purpose of circumcision in this context provides a better view of what was happening as God makes His promise with Abraham. God makes clear that this is for "you and your descendants" and that they would all equally share the burden of *keeping the faith* for generations to come.

For God's covenant with Abraham was not with him alone, but with his entire household, for all of his children, whoever and wherever they may be, for all generations to come. And so, as God makes this promise with Abraham, He is declaring that this promise is extended to all who have the right to be called his children.

> *Yet to all who did receive [Jesus], to those who believed in his name, he gave the right to become children of God—children born not of natural descent, nor of human decision or a husband's will, but born of God.*
>
> JOHN 1:12-13 NIV

> *Abraham was, humanly speaking, the founder of our Jewish nation. What did he discover about being made right with God? If his good deeds had made him acceptable to God, he would have had something to boast about. But that was not God's way. For the Scriptures tell us, "Abraham believed God, and God counted him as righteous because of his faith."*
>
> ROMANS 4:1-3 NLT

> *For I am not ashamed of this Good News about Christ. It is the power of God at work, saving everyone who believes–the Jew first and also the Gentile. This Good News tells us how God makes us right in his sight. This is accomplished from start to finish by faith. As the Scriptures say, "It is through faith that a righteous person has life."*
>
> ROMANS 1:16-17 NLT

Circumcision became a mark of the covenant between God and all of Abraham's descendants. Women didn't require circumcision because, culturally, they represented the men in their households and clans. A woman didn't live a "single" life, and so she was directly connected to her father's household (or clan) until such a time as she married, at which point she became "one" with her husband's identity. So, as each male in Abraham's household was circumcised (remember, Abraham was a hundred years old now and had a lot of servant [employee] families traveling with him), each of those individual families also became heirs to the promise, now marked as part of Abraham's tribe, and representatives of the promise.

A KINGDOM COME

Effectively, God was marking the boundaries for His kingdom. As we accept God to be the king of the universe and sovereign over all creation, we can easily accept that the entire universe is indeed God's kingdom. But what God is doing here with Abraham is something different, something unique. He is cutting a circle around a select group of individuals and marking them as sovereign and holy. God's position as king affords Him the right to set those boundaries as He sees fit. While He is most certainly king of all, nobody else in those days cared to respect His authority. And instead of ruling by force and oppression, He chose (and chooses) to lead with love.

"Now if you obey me fully and keep my covenant, then out of all nations you will be my treasured possession. Although the whole earth is mine, you will be for me a kingdom of priests and a holy nation."

Exodus 19:5-6 NIV

But you are a chosen people, a royal priesthood, a holy nation, God's special possession, that you may declare the praises of him who called you out of darkness into his wonderful light.

1 Peter 2:9 NIV

God was establishing a new monarchy, beginning with Abraham. Later, we watch as God increases His kingdom on earth and His perceived sovereignty among men, beginning with the Exodus and continuing through the taking of the Promised Land as recorded in the book of Joshua.

But a kingdom was a very important reality. A kingdom included not only the land and everything in it, but also the people who lived in that land. Every individual who lived in that kingdom was under, not only the authority of the king but, the protection of the king. **Kneeling to the throne was not just an act of submission, but a recognition of the sovereignty and power of the king along with his leadership, authority and protection.** If the king doesn't protect the people, then he ultimately becomes just a land owner. A kingdom, therefore, is not the land but rather the citizens who occupy it.

When a king's subjects maintained a fear of the throne, they displayed honor and respect. The people of a good king did not live in fear of punishment, but rather lived in fear of being put out of the kingdom if they failed to adhere to the doctrine and lordship of its head. Because being cast out of the kingdom meant that you were no longer under the protection of the crown. You would be on your own, disavowed, and no longer a recipient of the privileges granted to those belonging to that kingdom.

If you did not claim fealty to the king, then you did not belong to the king, and you could not look to the king or his men to protect you or your family.

That is why those who rule with terror rule very fragile kingdoms indeed. As we know from history and experience, those who are oppressed have no sincere loyalty to their oppressors. If those who are supposed to protect you cause you harm, then you can only bide your time until an opportunity to leave (or overthrow) them becomes available. But a king who rules with honor and justice and love is to be revered and given praise. A king who cherishes the people more than the land they occupy is a very good king. This is the kingdom of God.

And so God was declaring to Abraham that he and his descendants were going to be the foundation of this new kingdom. They would be His people, and He would be their King. As Christians, we are subjects of that same kingdom. Yet only if we keep the promise.

As the apostolic letters of the New Testament state, and as we've noted previously, it is not by physical ancestry that believers in Christ are considered children of Abraham. As Christians, we are not children of Abraham by blood, but are children of the promise itself. Just like those who were considered part of Abraham's physical household by being marked through circumcision, we too are considered part of Abraham's spiritual household by means of our faith, marked by the Holy Spirit.

> *We have been saying that Abraham's faith was credited to him as righteousness. Under what circumstances was it credited? Was it after he was circumcised, or before? It was not after, but before! And he received circumcision as a sign, a seal of the righteousness that he had by faith while he was still uncircumcised. So then, he is the father of all who believe but have not been circumcised, in order that righteousness might be credited to them. And he is then also the father of the circumcised who not only are circumcised but who also follow*

in the footsteps of the faith that our father Abraham had before he was circumcised . . .

Therefore, the promise comes by faith, so that it may be by grace and may be guaranteed to all Abraham's offspring—not only to those who are of the law but also to those who have the faith of Abraham. He is the father of us all.

ROMANS 4:9-12, 16 NIV

Paul tells us here that we are children of the promise by our faith in Jesus Christ. It is that faith that God credits to us as righteousness—before we have performed any action whatsoever, be it circumcision or baptism, or any other action a local community may demand. In the days of Abraham, though he was the only one with faith, his entire household was included in the promise. God did not require that everyone else in his family had faith too, but only that they "keep the covenant" by being circumcised and remaining obedient to Abraham as the head of their household, just as God was Abraham's head (and as Christ is the head of the Church). What God required was obedience. That alone was God's expectation, and His promise for a great blessing.

When you came to Christ, you were "circumcised," but not by a physical procedure. Christ performed a spiritual circumcision—the cutting away of your sinful nature.

COLOSSIANS 2:11 NLT

In this chapter, I've drawn a few parallels between circumcision and baptism to demonstrate the relationship of one to the other. And while there are many similarities of function and purpose, they are most certainly not the same. In the passage above, Paul makes clear to us that we each undergo "spiritual circumcision" when we come to Christ, and not as a result of any later physical act. Like Abraham, we are justified by faith before any action we can possibly take. But, like circumcision, baptism appears to be a sign of our covenant with God, yet after He has already declared us to be "righteous" as the blood of Jesus washes over us.

The Original Detox Program
Chapter 7: Washing Away the Past

ISAIAH **44:3 NIV**

PURIFICATION IS THE PROCESS of removing contaminants and unwanted materials from something. Heat or fire is frequently used to purify metals, and the distillation process makes the resulting evaporated and collected water "pure" by leaving most other non-water molecules behind. This is the same natural process that converts salty ocean water into the clouds that drop fresh rainwater back onto the earth (in theory).

In the context of washing, of course, we typically do our best to start with water from a "clean" or uncontaminated source and use that to wash away any impurities that may be present on the fruits or vegetables we eat, and to wash away the contaminants we know are present on nearly every surface. And we use (waste, actually) lots and lots of water to wash away the impurities that are excreted from and collected on our own bodies throughout each day.

Ironically, we know that even the purest form of water is not pure, as it contains all the varying particulates it collects on its journey from the ground to the heavens and back again.

But washing isn't quite the same as purification, even though their purpose is very similar. When we wash something, we're basically attempting to make it suitable for some purpose by removing what's on the outside.

We wash fresh vegetables so that we don't contaminate our bodies with the soil, insects and chemicals that may be present on their surfaces. We wash our hands and our bodies so that the dirt, oil, sweat, and bacteria that form and collect on our skin and in our hair doesn't build up or transfer onto our clothes, our sheets, or onto others we come in contact with (plus, we smell better!). The purpose of washing is to minimize transfer of contaminants. But, of course, this is only superficial, as our bodies, especially, can get rather filthy even if we never leave our homes—or our beds.

But being "unclean" is not the same as being dirty. As Jesus notes below, washing only handles the dirt on the outside. Being unclean is an internal or conditional issue that washing just can't fix.

> *"Woe to you, experts in the law and you Pharisees, hypocrites! You clean the outside of the cup and the dish, but inside they are full of greed and self-indulgence. Blind Pharisee! First clean the inside of the cup, so that the outside may become clean too! Woe to you, experts in the law and you Pharisees, hypocrites! You are like whitewashed tombs that look beautiful on the outside but inside are full of the bones of the dead and of everything unclean."*
> MATTHEW 23:27 NET

Unlike washing, purification is a process. Instead of being concerned with what's on the outside, purification is about cleaning what's on the inside.

Because the definition of uncleanness can differ from one to another, and from purpose to purpose, the process of purification, or cleansing, can involve many different things depending on what you're attempting to achieve, and what your standard of purification is.

For example, when we're washing our vegetables prior to cooking or consumption, running tap water is usually sufficient, because we believe that the running water is enough to magically loosen and remove the unwanted dirt and microscopic creatures that may be present on their surfaces. Well, when we're "rinsing" bell peppers, we can easily tell that the dirt is gone and there are no visible insects. But what about broccoli or leafy greens? Does holding them under the faucet for a few seconds do the job? Or is some more advanced method of rinsing required? What is the purpose of the washing?

You see, that purpose must be known in advance in order to effectively accomplish that purpose through any determined process. But if we don't understand its purpose, why should the process—traditional or otherwise—matter?

Today, one may practice a physical "purification" or *cleanse*, wherein the process of cleansing takes place over a period of time. During that time, a person may consume only certain liquids, especially water, and maybe other specific foods that cause the human body to expel unwanted substances considered to be toxic or unhealthy. This process usually takes several days or weeks for the purification, or detoxification, to be considered complete.

THE CLEANSE

The earliest appearance of the term *letaher* (*lĕ-taw-hĕr´*, *Hebrew*—to cleanse or purify) in the Old Testament occurs in Genesis. Jacob's clan has just left the city of Shechem (Jacob is the grandson of Abraham). After they arrived in Shechem weeks earlier, Jacob's daughter Dinah was raped by the ruler's son. When her brothers found out about it, they responded by slaughtering all the men in that city and plundering it, taking many of the women and children with them.

After they finished there, God tells Jacob to go to a place called

Bethel and build an altar to Him for all that He had demonstrated to Jacob up to that point. In those days, the LORD was not the only god believed to be around, and people continued to worship many things, including the various workers and servants in Jacob's own household. (No, people didn't worship the workers and servants, I mean that the workers and servants worshiped other gods.)

> *Then God said to Jacob, "Go up to Bethel and settle there, and build an altar there to God, who appeared to you when you were fleeing from your brother Esau."*
>
> *So Jacob said to his household and to all who were with him, "Get rid of the foreign gods you have with you, and purify yourselves and change your clothes. Then come, let us go up to Bethel, where I will build an altar to God, who answered me in the day of my distress and who has been with me wherever I have gone." So they gave Jacob all the foreign gods they had and the rings in their ears, and Jacob buried them under the oak at Shechem.*
>
> GENESIS 35:1-4 NIV

Before they even headed out to their destination, Jacob commanded everyone in his household to abandon everything that indicated loyalty to anything besides his God. So the people gave up all of their cast idols, jewelry and trinkets, and removed any rings they had in their ears.

Earrings were often symbols, not of stature, but of servitude. An earring showed devotion to another, and so were considered idolatrous. Whether the earrings the servants wore were representative of the polytheistic gods of the day or were intended only as cosmetic, they indicated a devotion to other gods, other matters, or to self.

Jacob was making a statement. Jacob was declaring that his household would be God-followers, beginning right there, right then. So everyone unburdened themselves of everything that connected them to their pasts. That day was a new day, and all things were being made new.

It's important to understand here that Jacob's household most certainly included his eleven sons, his daughter, and all four of their mothers, along with each of his children's families, plus all their servants, their servants' families, livestock and possessions. And, of course, his household now included all the women and children they had quite recently plundered from the city of Shechem detailed in the previous chapter (of the Bible, not this book).

Not only was this huge group commanded to expunge their worldly possessions, but they were to also "purify themselves" (spiritually) and change their clothes. They were starting over, it would seem—perhaps even washing themselves with water—for the purpose of metaphorically removing the physical remnants of their past idolatries (or servitude) and moving forward into their new lives, foreshadowing his descendants' exodus through the Red Sea, with the "pledge of a clear conscience toward God" (1 Peter 3:21).

For many, however, the issue may not be what we are changing into, but what we are changing out of. **For it is not the new that frightens us, but the abandoning of the familiar.**

So for this purpose, a true physical washing was not required (though implied). Instead, only ritualistic purification was needed, one that transformed their hearts and their minds into a new way of thinking and living. And it's this new way of thinking that draws us closer to God via our relationship with Jesus, our Teacher . . . our *Master.* So, as we see, this idea of *putting off the old* is not a Christian concept.

THE BLOOD OF PURIFICATION

Several generations and many years later, during the Exodus, God gave instructions to Moses for consecrating Aaron and the other Levites (the tribe of Levi) who would serve as priests, then and in the future.

> *"Then bring Aaron and his sons to the entrance to the tent of meeting and wash them with water . . . Take the anointing oil and anoint him by pouring it on his head . . . Slaughter [a bull] and take the blood and splash it against the sides of the altar . . . Sacrifice a bull each day as a sin offering to make atonement. Purify the altar by making atonement for it, and anoint it to consecrate it."*
>
> EXODUS 29:4, 7, 16, 36 NIV

As we noted earlier, purification is a process. Here, God is prescribing a specific process through which ordained priests would be considered sufficient for service. This process involved washing with water (the outside), anointing with oil (an official symbol, though invisible), and the shedding of life's blood, splashed (aspersed) upon the altar, as an atonement for sin.

This part of the process was initially conceived on the evening of the original Passover, of course, in the twilight hour when the Israelites slaughtered lambs and spread the blood on the doorframes of their homes. Through their obedience, they were all spared that night from the tragic death of every firstborn child in Egypt.

As Christians, we know that Jesus became our Passover Lamb once for all, and that "if we walk in the light, as he is in the light, we have fellowship with one another, and the blood of Jesus, his Son, purifies us from all sin" (1 John 1:7 NIV).

And so the purification of the priests at that time was extremely important, hence the requirement that each priest be properly purified and prepared for service. This is because the priests were responsible for representing the entire people of Israel. The priests were the only ones who were permitted to enter the inner parts of the temple, and God's presence, to offer the required sacrifices on behalf of the people. The priests served as intercessors, as the people were not permitted to offer their own sacrifices.

Priesthood was a position of extreme responsibility, and therefore of great notoriety and nobility (and it's easy to see how it got corrupted over several hundred years). But because of that responsibility, their position carried the highest degree of requirement and accountability. And any priest who skipped even the smallest step in the process was found by God to be unworthy and put to death immediately. God's requirements were clear, and His judgment was swift.

> *Moses and Aaron then entered into the Meeting Tent. When they came out, they blessed the people, and the glory of the* LORD *appeared to all the people. Then fire went out from the presence of the* LORD *and consumed the burnt offering and the fat parts on the altar, and all the people saw it, so they shouted loudly and fell down with their faces to the ground. Then Aaron's sons, Nadab and Abihu, each took his fire pan and put fire in it, set incense on it, and presented strange fire before the* LORD*, which he had not commanded them to do. So fire went out from the presence of the* LORD *and consumed them so that they died before the* LORD*.*
>
> LEVITICUS 9:23-10:2 NET

They failed to purify themselves, so God did it for them.

It is here we can see the connection between the deeds required by Judaism (the Law) to be made right before God, and the consequences of having to live according to that law. For, as Paul tells us, if we choose to live according to the law (and judge others accordingly), then God will judge us according to that same law, and we will be found guilty.

> *For by the standard you judge you will be judged, and the measure you use will be the measure you receive.*
>
> MATTHEW 7:2 NET

> *Obviously, the law applies to those to whom it was given, for its purpose is to keep people from having excuses, and to show that the entire world is guilty before God. For no one can ever be made right with God by doing what the law commands. The law simply shows us how sinful we are.*
>
> Romans 3:19-20 NLT

But the Good News is that we are made right with God, not by our own merits—not because we deserve rightness with God as a result of our efforts and conformity to the law, but in spite of our inability to keep the law.

> *But now God has shown us a way to be made right with him without keeping the requirements of the law, as was promised in the writings of Moses and the prophets long ago. We are made right with God by placing our faith in Jesus Christ. And this is true for everyone who believes, no matter who we are.*
>
> Romans 3:21-22 NET

The Apprenticeship
Chapter 8: Changing Your Stars

CONFORMING TO NEW GUIDELINES and a new way of life or purpose, as demonstrated by Jacob and his household, cannot be accomplished while one attempts to hang on to his past or even do "a little bit" of his own thing. For when one is willing to follow the leadership of another, even if that means simply going along with *their* purpose (since it's common that one has yet to discover his own), there must still be a change in position, attitude, and behavior.

First, one must agree to go along with this new leadership. Then he must adjust his attitude and be willing to be obedient to this new leadership. Finally, he must actually go along with the program and practice obedience.

In our western culture, Christians don't necessarily grasp the true purpose of discipleship nor understand the historical and cultural significance of it. It's often viewed as a general partnership between believers, like that relationship between a recovering alcoholic and his sponsor (who then has his own sponsor, and so on . . .).

But in Jewish culture, a *rabbi* ("master" or "teacher") is one who is significantly versed in Torah, its understanding, and its application. Rabbis were indeed considered masters of their craft, which was of being wise, learned, and of living a life that most represented how God wanted people to live, according to the Law, with the purpose of drawing them to Himself.

Around the world and for thousands of years, an apprentice wanting to learn a trade would often move in with a master craftsman and spend years under his tutelage. My favorite example of this is seen in the 2001 film, *A Knight's Tale*, starring Heath Ledger.[29]

Near the climax of the film, we reflect on our hero William's (Ledger) childhood to a day when, as a small peasant boy, his father sends him off to apprentice under a knight in a faraway land. His father expects never to see his son again, but hopes that, under the instruction of this master, his son could one day grow to be worthy of knighthood. For there was no illusion or expectation that young William could ever become a knight, since that could be accomplished only by birth (nobility) and not by any ambition or by works.

Over the course of that apprenticeship, however, young William does grow up to become quite "knightly" indeed, having been raised under his master's instruction and training, with the story reaching a dramatic moment when young William does eventually "change his stars."

The crowned Prince Edward Colville (James Purefoy)—who himself attempted in vain to compete anonymously in several jousting competitions as a "common" knight—now finds William bound in the stocks for having criminally impersonated a knight. The prince approaches him and says:

> "What a pair we make, eh? Both trying to hide who we are, both unable to do so . . .
>
> "Your men love you. If I knew nothing else about you, that would be enough. But you also tilt when you should

---

29   *A Knight's Tale.* Columbia Pictures, Sony Pictures (2001).

withdraw . . . and that is knightly, too."

To the guards he commands, "Release him!"

As they unshackle him, the prince then turns to the gathered crowd and declares, "He may appear to be of humble origins, but my personal historians have discovered that he is descended from an ancient royal line. This is my word and, as such, is beyond contestation."

Turning back to William who is no longer in the stocks, Prince Edward says, "Now, if I may repay the kindness you once showed me . . . take a knee," and Edward draws his sword.

"By the power vested in me by my father, King Edward, and by all the witnesses here, I dub thee: Sir William!"

In this context, Prince Edward dubs William a knight by simply touching the flat surface of his sword to William's shoulder. However, we should recognize that it was not the sword that brought William into knighthood, nor was it specifically Prince Edward's words. But so the people could witness and acknowledge the prince's purpose, he performed this with ceremony for their benefit, and not in secret.

By this, William appears to have actually become a knight *before* the prince made it official. But when did his transformation into knighthood occur? It's impossible to tell, and we only know it happened somewhere between the prince's intention to make William a knight and his public declaration.

Of course, it's not hard to draw the parallel to what Jesus has done. We were imprisoned in our sin while trying to be something we were not, or ever could be. But then, at just the right time, the Prince comes, not just to free us from our prison, but to elevate us by declaring us righteous, and setting us apart as special.

The term *apprentice* is formed from the same root as "apprehend" (Latin *apprehendere*), meaning "to grasp or lay hold of." To grasp the learning necessary to one day master a trade, this often meant moving in and literally[30] walking in his master's shoes. But since the master would only work for a limited number of hours each day, the apprentice would ultimately be involved in all aspects of the master's household. The apprentice would effectively become a member of the household, performing chores and menial tasks, serving the master as might a slave. In fact, it might be months (or years, depending on the age of the apprentice) before he was even given the opportunity to begin working with his master at his trade.

This immersion into his master's life was paramount to the apprentice's learning. It was once said that, "You cannot separate life from work. The way you do the most insignificant activity in your daily life will reflect in your work" (Anonymous). As a result of this immersion into his master's life and trade, the apprentice would learn over time *why* the master did what he did and what caused him to make the choices he made in his work. Since the work the master performed was indeed a reflection of his own character, **the apprentice had to first learn to reflect the character of his master.** Only then could the apprentice become a craftsman.

This is discipleship. As Christians, it is God's intention that we would walk with Jesus—our Rabbi, for "by this we know that we are in him. The one who says he resides in God ought himself to walk just as Jesus walked" (1 John 2:5-6 NET).

This idea of apprenticeship is at the heart of Jesus' selection of the dozen specific followers He chose to be His apostles. These twelve men (known affectionately as *The Twelve*) walked in His shoes for nearly three years (they were always wearing each other's sandals), coming to understand why Jesus did and said what He did. Ultimately (except for the one who decided on a career change), all of these apprentices became prepared and equipped to serve as *masters* to all new believers, apprenticing others to take their places when their respective times had come.

---

30   This literally means *figuratively.*

And it is this same theme we see played out in the Old Testament book of 1 Kings at the calling of Elisha, a young man who would succeed Elijah as the prophet of God:

> *The LORD said to [Elijah], "Go back the way you came, and go to the Desert of Damascus. When you get there, anoint Hazael king over Aram. Also, anoint Jehu son of Nimshi king over Israel, and anoint Elisha son of Shaphat from Abel Meholah to succeed you as prophet . . .*
>
> *So Elijah went from there and found Elisha son of Shaphat. He was plowing with twelve yoke of oxen, and he himself was driving the twelfth pair. Elijah went up to him and threw his cloak around him. Elisha then left his oxen and ran after Elijah. "Let me kiss my father and mother goodbye," he said, "and then I will come with you."*
>
> *"Go back," Elijah replied. "What have I done to you?"*
>
> *So Elisha left him and went back. He took his yoke of oxen and slaughtered them. He burned the plowing equipment to cook the meat and gave it to the people, and they ate. Then he set out to follow Elijah and became his servant.*
>
> 1 KINGS 19:15-16, 19-21 NIV

The idea of "burning your ships" and leaving everything behind alludes to certain famous, though likely allegorical, incidents where an armed forces commander would order his men to destroy their ships, preventing them from retreating and going back the way they came. They would have to move forward or die. There was no going back. Such stories seem to stem from this biblical account, and it is this reference to the calling of Elisha to which Jesus is referring when He tells a potential follower,

> *"No one who puts a hand to the plow and looks back is fit for service in the kingdom of God."*
>
> LUKE 9:62 NET

Eddie Davidson explains, "You can't plow looking back over where you've been. You'll end up plowing a crooked row and potentially damage existing plants. Once you put your hand to the plow of following Jesus, if you look back, you will live a crooked, tentative life. Plowing requires a single-minded focus, and so does following Jesus."[31]

Therefore, before we kneel at the foot of the cross, we must indeed "count the cost" of following Him.

Large crowds were traveling with Jesus, and turning to them he said: "If anyone comes to me and does not hate father and mother, wife and children, brothers and sisters—yes, even their own life—such a person cannot be my disciple. And whoever does not carry their cross and follow me cannot be my disciple."

Luke 14:24-26 NIV

From this time many of his disciples turned back and no longer followed him. "You do not want to leave too, do you?" Jesus asked the Twelve. Simon Peter answered him, "Lord, to whom shall we go? You have the words of eternal life."

John 6:66-68 NIV

---

31   *Is Your Hand to the Plow?* by Eddie Davidson (March 2019).
     https://findsoulrest.com/2019/03/13/is-your-hand-to-the-plow/

Clean or Unclean?
That is the Question
Chapter 9: Can't Touch This!

Now God had ordained that, under certain circumstances, people, animals, and other objects could be considered unclean. This concept of cleanness and uncleanness was a matter of status for every member of the community. Anyone considered to be unclean was to be excluded from a number of (if not most) social activities, including basic fellowship, and they were most certainly forbidden from approaching or touching anything that was considered clean or holy.

When one was ceremonially clean, he or she was in normal fellowship with the community and with God. Everyone went about their daily lives, concerned mainly with doing what was right and their own need for atonement according to the law. But in order for one to remain clean, one could not come into contact, directly or indirectly, with something or someone that was unclean.

Such things could be certain kinds of animals, or people with infectious skin diseases. Quite commonly, however, uncleanness occurred as a result from contact with blood or having a bodily discharge (ew!), especially a woman's menstrual bleeding via her normal monthly cycle or as a result of childbirth, or from contact with anyone else who had or came in contact with such a discharge. Of course, part of life was "death", and uncleanness would also occur after touching a dead body or animal (a carcass, not as food), which sometimes could not be helped; but was always the result of contact with something external and rarely something within a person's control. As such, being unclean was never a *spiritual* issue, it was just a condition of daily life that had to be contended with. It was not a sin, so in most cases no sacrifice was required. And because these types of things were all relatively normal (short of the skin diseases and dead bodies), there was normally no great shame associated with becoming unclean, and everyone just followed the prescribed purification process required for the given circumstance.[32]

This meant that, in the normal course of daily living, everyone was at risk of becoming unclean at one point or another. And while it was certainly normal, being unclean could be a significant and inconvenient social issue. For the casual substance-toucher, it was kind of a secret. When there was a bodily discharge of any sort, the individual would wash (of course), put on clean clothes, wash their soiled ones (and anything else they came in contact with), and then wait until evening when the new day began.[33]

Then they were good to go. Nobody outside the home would really know, though they might speculate:

> "Hey, where's Joey today?"
> "I don't know . . . maybe he had a discharge."

But other circumstances were a bit more obvious, and the resulting uncleanness could last some time. And so being unclean could be very problematic. You couldn't *go* anywhere or really *do* anything because anyone or anything you touched, directly or indirectly, would also become unclean.

Imagine, if you can, a *pandemic*, where every precaution was

---

32 *Mishnah Mikvaot.*
    https://www.sefaria.org/Mishnah_Mikvaot.1

33 *Ceremonial Washing and the Mikveh* by Ceil Rosen (July 2007).
    https://jewsforjesus.org/publications/issues/issues-v02-n10/baptism-pagan-or-jewish/

taken to ensure one did not transmit an illness that could be easily spread by contact or close proximity. You couldn't go to church, and you couldn't be around others. You were isolated, cutoff from extended family, the community, and from worship. As a result, anyone who was unclean and outside their home was considered untouchable. No hugs, no kisses, no conversation, and no social contact. Hard to imagine, I know.

Abnormal feminine bleeding and skin diseases were the worst because they were not especially normal (hence the term "abnormal") plus they were visible. Neither were they conditions that could be easily concealed, and so afflicted individuals were outcast.[34]

> *And a woman was there who had been subject to bleeding for twelve years. She had suffered a great deal under the care of many doctors and had spent all she had, yet instead of getting better she grew worse. When she heard about Jesus, she came up behind him in the crowd and touched his cloak, because she thought, "If I just touch his clothes, I will be healed." Immediately her bleeding stopped and she felt in her body that she was freed from her suffering.*
>
> MARK 5:25-29 NIV

Like leprosy (although the skin diseases represented as leprosy in the Bible weren't always leprosy), such conditions were not readily treatable by doctors. So they were things people just had to live with. They prayed for healing, but it didn't always come, **because their affliction wasn't necessarily what was keeping them from a relationship with God.**

> *As [Jesus] was going into a village, ten men who had leprosy met him. They stood at a distance and called out in a loud voice, "Jesus, Master, have pity on us!" When he saw them,*

---

34 *Leviticus and the Law of Bodily Discharges.* Got Questions Ministries (November 2016). https://www.gotquestions.org/bodily-discharge.html

> *he said, "Go, show yourselves to the priests." And as they went,
> they were cleansed. One of them, when he saw he was healed,
> came back, praising God in a loud voice. He threw himself at
> Jesus' feet and thanked him—and he was a Samaritan. Jesus
> asked, "Were not all ten cleansed? Where are the other
> nine? Has no one returned to give praise to God except this
> foreigner?" Then he said to him, "Rise and go; your faith has
> made you well."*
>
> LUKE 17:12-19 NIV

We often make promises to God in exchange for healing (physical or otherwise), as if He is obliged to engage in such a conditional deal. But our relationship with Him cannot be a condition of our circumstances, or of His performance, since His relationship with us is most certainly not conditional on our performance.[35]

Anyway, water was instrumental in every prescription for ritual purification. Moving from a state of uncleanness to cleanness usually just involved washing your body, your clothes, and some period of time; though, as I mentioned, sometimes a sacrifice was also required.

Overall, being unclean really was a big deal in Jewish culture. Washing and changing your clothes, not so much. But as long as you were unclean, you could not really be around others, and you most certainly couldn't be around that which was holy. That meant until you had become clean again, you were out of relationship with God. For He declared, "You are to be holy to me because I, the Lord, am holy, and I have set you apart from the nations to be my own" (Leviticus 20:26). Therefore, it was an ongoing requirement that the people observed all of the requirements for remaining so. Coming in contact with things or others that were ceremonially unclean made that individual unclean and separated him or her from God's fellowship until

---

35   *With: Reimagining the Way You Relate to God,* by Skye Jethani (Thomas Nelson, 2011).

their purification was complete.

However, while touching someone or something unclean caused that person to become unclean, the water used for the purification of that person did not become unclean. For as we'll see, the water itself acted as the catalyst for purification. And because Jesus is also the "Living Water" (more on this later), **He was and is able to continually "cleanse" others without becoming unclean Himself.**

Now, in some cases of purification, additional time was also required. For example, after giving birth to a boy, a woman remained unclean for a week and then had to wait thirty-three days before she could come near the sanctuary to worship (two weeks/sixty-six days following the birth of a girl, since they're twice as dirty): [36]

> *Now when the days of [Mary's] purification according to the law of Moses were completed, they brought [Jesus] to Jerusalem to present Him to the Lord (as it is written in the law of the Lord, "Every male who opens the womb shall be called holy to the Lord"), and to offer a sacrifice according to what is said in the law of the Lord, "a pair of turtledoves or two young pigeons."*
> LUKE 2:22-24 NKJV

Ultimately, the purpose of purification in this context was to bring one from a state of impurity, or *tumah (tĕ-maw´)*, to a state of purity, or *taharah (tĕ-hĕr´-ah)*. While God declared the Israelites to be holy because He "makes them holy," He also provided a requirement for them to recognize His superior holiness and revere Him by never attempting to approach Him when they were in an impure or unclean state.

Likewise, Aaron and all those who belonged to the tribe of Levi, who were designated as priests, were required to be ritually clean before approaching the altar for service or entering the tent

---

36   *See Leviticus 12:1-8*

of meeting (the place where God's presence resides):

> *Then the L*ORD *said to Moses, "Make a bronze basin, with its bronze stand, for washing. Place it between the tent of meeting and the altar, and put water in it. Aaron and his sons are to wash their hands and feet with water from it. Whenever they enter the tent of meeting, they shall wash with water so that they will not die. Also, when they approach the altar to minister by presenting a food offering to the L*ORD*, they shall wash their hands and feet so that they will not die. This is to be a lasting ordinance for Aaron and his descendants for the generations to come."*
>
> EXODUS 30:17-21 NIV

THE ORAL TORAH

While the Bible itself does not specifically state the differences or requirements when it mentions washing or cleansing, we must keep in mind that God's instructions to the Israelites included a little more than just what was written down on scrolls. In those days, many of the details of the law were communicated orally.

The idea of this oral *torah* is the same as classroom instruction needed to explain and prepare students according to what is found in their math textbooks. The textbook provides mathematical laws and theorems, but understanding how to apply those laws in the real world requires examples and added information from the instructor. This is also analogous to a judge's ability to interpret the law for each unique application, and her ability to apply sound judgment accordingly. In fact, the term *torah*, commonly translated "law" in most English Bibles, is more accurately rendered "instruction" or "teaching." This is best understood in the following passage taken from the Common English Bible:

> *The truly happy person doesn't follow wicked advice, doesn't stand on the road of sinners, and doesn't sit with the disrespectful. Instead of doing those things, these persons love the Lord's Instruction [torah], and they recite God's Instruction day and night! They are like a tree replanted by streams of water, which bears fruit at just the right time and whose leaves don't fade. Whatever they do succeeds.*
>
> PSALM 1:1-3 CEB

But the oral *torah* included all of the instruction given to Moses, Aaron and the elders that wasn't written down. Initially, other than the Ten Commandments, nothing was written down until Moses wrote it down, which could have taken years. Certainly, the Israelites didn't sit around waiting for Moses to finish writing before implementing everything.

When the priests were commanded to sacrifice an animal when making a particular atonement, the instructions on just precisely how to sacrifice that animal was not to be found in the scrolls, but through the teaching of one priest to another over time.[37] When we look at the time of Moses and the exodus, we see the elders from each clan being given those same instructions:

> *So Moses returned from the mountain and called together the elders of the people and told them everything the LORD had commanded him.*
>
> EXODUS 19:7 NIV

---

37 *Babylonian Talmud.* After the destruction of the temple in Jerusalem in AD 70, a collection of leading rabbis determined to put these oral teachings and commentaries into writing so that centuries of instruction would not be lost. These efforts are now known as the Midrash and the Talmud. To the Orthodox Jew, these collective works, along with the first five books of the Old Testament, represent the entire Torah. However, it's important to note that what has been written and compiled into these books has no evidentiary support, serving only to maintain the traditions of classical rabbinical teaching, and is never presented as God's Word. This is no different than the Catholic Church that holds more firmly to the writings and commentary of early Church writers (opinions) than to the New Testament gospels and letters themselves.

> *Then the LORD instructed Moses: "Come up here to me, and bring along Aaron, Nadab, Abihu, and seventy of Israel's elders. All of you must worship from a distance.*
>
> EXODUS 24:1 NIV

However, even this oral instruction remains just "instruction." The interpretation of Scripture remains as such, allowing much discussion and debate of the application of the Law amongst scholars.

THE RITUAL BATH

Looking at Exodus 30 again, we see that the priests were required to wash in the bronze basin they made for that purpose. However, the text doesn't indicate the specifics of the basin, or the water source that was to be used. The basin was to be elevated (on a bronze stand), but its exact construction and height is not mentioned.

The water was not to be stagnant, of course, nor the priests able to simply "dip" their hands into it for sufficiency. The water in the basin, or any gathered location (or *mikveh*) had its own requirements. The idea is that water, by nature, is clean and pure from its source. But once pooled or "gathered", and the longer it sits without movement or change, the less acceptable it becomes.[38]

* There are six degrees of gatherings of water, each superior to the other.

* The water of pits . . . The same rules apply to the water of pits, the water of cisterns, the water of ditches, the water of caverns, the water of rain drippings which have stopped, and mikveh of less than forty seahs: they are all clean during the time of rain; when the rain has stopped those near to a city or to a road are

---

38 *English Explanation of Mishnah Mikvaot.* Dr. Joshua Kulp.
https://www.sefaria.org/English_Explanation_of_Mishnah_Mikvaot.1.1

unclean, and those distant remain clean until the majority of people pass [that way].

* Superior to such is the water of rain drippings which have not stopped.

* Superior to such is the mikveh containing forty seahs (about 300 liters), for in it persons may immerse themselves and immerse others.

* Superior again is a fountain whose own water is little but has been increased by a greater quantity of drawn water; it is equivalent to the mikveh inasmuch as it may render clean by standing water, and to an [ordinary] fountain inasmuch as one may immerse in it whatever the quantity of its contents.

* Superior again are "smitten waters" which can render clean even when flowing.

* Superior again are "living waters" which serve for the immersion of persons who have a running issue and for the sprinkling of lepers, and are valid for the preparation of the water of purification.

And it's this last entry that catches our eye. So let's take a closer look at why this *living water* was so important.

Sometimes You Have to Stir Things Up

Chapter 10: So Let's Keep Things Moving

COMMON SENSE TELLS US that moving water is "fresher" than still water, certainly more so than stagnant water. The more recently the water has moved or stirred, the more potable it is, and the better for use in any application. Animals, by nature, when approaching a still body of water, first attempt to detect any problems with it by smell. If it passes that test, often a very small tongue taste is used to confirm its drinkability. If the water is not safe, it is avoided entirely (unless the animal is dying of thirst . . . or is suicidal).

Even beyond the purpose of consumption, a preference for "water in motion" is always perceived as superior. In the old west (and several other points on an old compass), water troughs were frequently placed beside pumps (from a well) that allowed fresh water to be pumped into them, mixing the newly drawn water with what was already present. That's because water drawn from a well was typically less susceptible to contamination, as it was already "bubbling up" through the rock and soil that provided natural, if only rudimentary, filtration.

Where people did not live near a lake, river or stream, they would create large collectors, or cisterns, designed for the catching of rainwater and storing it indefinitely. This was especially common in ancient times, but such systems are still in use today in rural areas where there is no fresh water source nearby. The larger the cistern, the longer the water could be considered "fresh." And those that maintained cisterns knew then that by the regular stirring of the tanks the water could remain potable indefinitely. For those who did live near a lake, the water there was always considered fresh simply because of the sheer volume of water it contained. Smaller pools of surface water were questionable.

But those who were fortunate enough to live by a stream or river (though I suspect luck had nothing to do with it) generally had the freshest water of all. When we consider the "circle of life" of fresh water, we can begin with snow (or other sky borne versions of it) falling onto mountaintops. As the snow melts, the near-freezing water passes over and through various rocks and minerals underground as it travels to the sea, going through a process of filtration as well as gaining some mineral enrichment. Because the water is moving, it's a less conducive environment for microorganisms to flourish. As a "rolling stone gathers no moss," so living water gathers no death.

Superfood guru Darin Olien explains, "There's no such thing as 'pure' water. It's all tea . . . When [water] comes from unpolluted springs, it has been exposed to oxygen due to its movement through the earth. As it rushes over rocks and dirt, it picks up minerals and salts. The sunlight infuses it with healing energy. Movement, minerals, and the sun all structure water naturally, making it more biologically harmonious to our cells and body." [39]

Yet regardless of the quality or purity of the water, it is its most recent movement that concerns us. For even rushing water gathered from a muddy river is preferable to clear water taken from a still pond.

---

39   *Superlife.* Darin Olien, HarperWave; Reprint edition (December 2016)

A RIVER OF HOPE, A FOUNTAIN OF LIFE

The Hebrew word used for a ritual bath, *mikveh*, is defined as "hope, ground of hope, and things hoped for." But it can also mean a collection or gathering of something (such as water). And it shares the root *qavah (kaw-vaw')* which means "to wait or hope patiently for."[40]

> *O LORD, the [mikveh] of Israel, all who turn away from you will be disgraced. They will be buried in the dust of the earth, for they have abandoned the LORD, the fountain of living water.*
>
> JEREMIAH 17:13 NLT

Here, the prophet Jeremiah is crying out to God because all those to whom he has been directed to prophesy have rejected his words, and by definition, God's words. He says that those who turn away from God will become dried out, to be buried in the dust. This is because God, the "hope" of Israel, is the "fountain" of living water from which they are separating themselves. Apart from God, the people have no hope, and are nothing more than the dust of the earth from which they came.

> *[The upright] are like a tree replanted by streams of water, which bears fruit at just the right time and whose leaves don't fade. Whatever they do succeeds. That's not true for the wicked! They are like dust that the wind blows away.*
>
> PSALM 1:3-4 CEB

> *"His winnowing fork is in his hand to clear his threshing floor and to gather the wheat into his barn, but he will burn up the chaff with unquenchable fire."*
>
> LUKE 3:17 NIV

---

40   **mikveh** (*mik-vay'*)—*Hebrew*. Strong's Number 4723 Hebrew Concordance of the Old Testament. http://lexiconcordance.com/hebrew/4723.html

Those who "drink in" the Word of God (Jesus) stay connected to that Holy Fountain. Those who separate themselves from it are destined to "dry up" and return to the dust from which they are made. As we see the term *mikveh* show up throughout Scripture, we find this concept of "hope" and "waiting on the LORD" intrinsically linked to the living water of the Holy Spirit and its overflowing and everlasting spring.

And if we allow it, this pattern of hope can saturate our minds and transform the way we see the world. As our perspectives change, we learn to see others in a different light, providing us the ability to transform the way we interact and engage with them. As we begin to see things from a godly perspective through the lens of the Holy Spirit, we can more easily recognize others' flaws and failures as being either a need for Jesus or as a current "work-in-progress" of the Spirit of God. Meanwhile, we hope that others, in turn, see that we are a work-in-progress too.

> *Do not be conformed to this present world, but be transformed by the renewing of your mind, so that you may test and approve what is the will of God—what is good and well-pleasing and perfect.*
>
> ROMANS 12:2 NET

It is only through this shift in perspective that we can allow a transformation to take place. Many come to faith in Jesus Christ with the expectation that He will fix everything about them that's broken so that they can begin living out their new lives. However, those who fail to experience "magical" changes in their life—changes that fix the addiction, the failing marriage, the failing finances, etc.—can become angry and frustrated at God for not making it all better. But those who think this way fail to understand that God is not some genie in a bottle, but rather their Father—the Creator of the universe; their gentle, loving Father—who does not intrude on their freedoms. Instead, He always knocks before entering, waiting for us to "open the door" to our hearts so that He may be with us.

> *"Here I am! I stand at the door and knock. If anyone hears my voice and opens the door, I will come in and eat with that person, and they with me."*
> REVELATION 3:20 NIV

While some suggest this passage is telling non-believers to "open their heart" to God and accept Jesus, this verse is actually written to those who already believe. Here Jesus is saying that the Holy Spirit does not force His way into our hearts: we must receive Him. He will not make changes that we do not authorize. God may own our hearts, minds, souls and strength, but He has installed each of us as the Chief Executive Officers of our own lives. We are each one hundred percent "in charge" of what the Holy Spirit may or may not do within us. While He will most certainly advise us of those things that need correction (that we may become more like Him), He serves primarily as our Wonderful Counselor until such time as we authorize Him to act on our behalf.

> *For to us a child is born, to us a son is given, and the government will be on his shoulders. And he will be called Wonderful Counselor, Mighty God, Everlasting Father, Prince of Peace.*
> ISAIAH 9:6 NIV

Because, let's face it, we are obviously incapable of making those necessary changes on our own. If we could, would we not have already? If we could do it ourselves, we wouldn't need God's help! So why do we always seem to reach the point of needing God to fix it, and then refuse to let Him do so? Do we think He just stays in our house (since the last time we invited Him in) sweeping and cleaning and tidying up all the time like a live-in maid?

When we first receive the Holy Spirit, He comes to us with the desire to take up permanent residence. His desire is to move in and stay with us, partnering with us to grow us and His kingdom. Unfortunately, we've got our own "house rules", and His presence in our lives is usually rather conditional. Sure, He's welcome to stick around as long as He likes, just as long as He doesn't get in the way (or talk too much). *Make yourself at home, Jesus, just try to remember that this is* my *house! Don't be moving stuff around. I've got everything just how I like it!*

If we treat Him as a servant, that's the role He takes. And though He may seem content with doing so, this posture ties His hands so that He's not "allowed" to just fix things as needed. He most certainly must be asked (or invited) to make any changes. **And so, until we give Him such authorization, we make clear to Him that He is not even worthy of washing our feet.**

So now, when He does inform us of changes to be made in our lives, we must talk with Him about it, understand the purpose in it, and have a heart of repentance so that we can give Him permission to make those changes within us. Then, most importantly, we need to get out of the way! Instead, we often invite Him in to clean out and straighten up the closet, and then interrupt Him every ten minutes to throw some other piece of junk (or skeleton) in that same closet. Good grief! What's the deal with us?

> *What a wretched man I am! Who will rescue me from this body that is subject to death?*
> ROMANS 7:24 NIV

So before we allow ourselves to "choose" to let the Holy Spirit get to work, we must have the right perspective. And to gain the right perspective, we must first put on the correct lenses. To accomplish this, we must first learn to listen to the truth and tune out the lies. The Holy Spirit makes those differences clear to us, but we must "take captive every thought to make it obedient to Christ" (2 Corinthians 10:5). For only as we begin to think in our *right minds* can we discern the truth and allow ourselves to become obedient to Him.

And so, over time, the Holy Spirit—our Living Water—flows through us and refreshes us. This life-giving water makes us new by flushing out the impurities and making us holy. "By the power of the Holy Spirit" we are sanctified, justified, and reborn. While our transformation can occur only as quickly as we allow this water to flow, it never stops moving. And as each impurity gets flushed from our system, the more freely that water seems to go.

But long before that dam breaks and we figure everything else out, this Living Water rushes right over the top of our rocky hearts, splashing and "bubbling up" and getting others wet in the process. Although we know it will take a lifetime to cleanse us from all our impurities, we shouldn't prevent others from experiencing the thundering roar of the rapids!

> *Jesus answered, "Everyone who drinks this [well] water will be thirsty again, but whoever drinks the water I give them will never thirst. Indeed, the water I give them will become in them a spring of water welling up to eternal life."*
> JOHN 4:13-14 NIV

Perhaps it was this very statement by Jesus that was the basis for what would one day become a fantastic tale. It's possible that this biblical account became twisted over time, when eventually men in faraway lands began telling their own embellished stories of people being given new life, being born again, and gaining "immortality" as a result of coming into contact with this "living water."

Centuries later, legends would "spring forth" and take shape as the infamous and elusive Fountain of Youth[41] (for which Ponce de Leon is chiefly associated), as well as the medieval legend of Monty Python, I mean, King Arthur and his quest for the Holy

---

41   *Legends Revealed: Ponce de Leon & The Fountain of Youth.* Mattison Hansen (April 2022) https://gargoyle.flagler.edu/2022/04/legends-revealed-ponce-de-leon-the-fountain-of-youth

Grail (What? Ridden on a horse?).[42]

THE RED SEA

Back in the days of Moses and the writing of the Old Testament, we find the Israelite nation being brought up out of Egypt after four hundred and thirty years of slavery (Exodus 12:41). Instead of taking the fast way out of town, however, God led the Israelites south from the land of Goshen down to where they would appear "cornered" by Pharaoh and the Egyptian army, at a point near what is now the Straits of Tiran (between the Sinai and Arabian peninsulas).

Even though Pharaoh (Egypt's king) had been convinced (after ten catastrophic plagues) to let God's people go out into the wilderness so that they could go and worship their God, Pharaoh changed his mind and began to pursue them.

It was there at the Red Sea that God gave a magnificent display of power, bringing nearly two and a half million people and their livestock across the sea floor on solid dry ground, keeping them from having to sludge through a muddy and slippery path. (This is the most under-acknowledged part of this whole event. Not that the water was walled up on either side to make a way, but that God completely dried up the ground for them to walk on.) For what would take several hours (all night), many of the Israelites were just beginning to step out onto the opposite shore as the last of their pack were just walking into the seabed.

> Then the Egyptians—all of Pharaoh's horses, chariots, and charioteers—chased them into the middle of the sea. But just before dawn the LORD looked down on the Egyptian army from the pillar of fire and cloud, and he threw their forces into total confusion. He twisted their chariot wheels, making their chariots difficult to drive. "Let's get out of here—away from

---

42   From *Monty Python and the Holy Grail.* Handmade Films; Python (Monty) Pictures Ltd. (1975)

these Israelites!" the Egyptians shouted. "The LORD is fighting for them against Egypt!"

When all the Israelites had reached the other side, the LORD said to Moses, "Raise your hand over the sea again. Then the waters will rush back and cover the Egyptians and their chariots and charioteers." So as the sun began to rise, Moses raised his hand over the sea, and the water rushed back into its usual place. The Egyptians tried to escape, but the LORD swept them into the sea. Then the waters returned and covered all the chariots and charioteers—the entire army of Pharaoh. Of all the Egyptians who had chased the Israelites into the sea, not a single one survived.

But the people of Israel had walked through the middle of the sea on dry ground, as the water stood up like a wall on both sides. That is how the LORD rescued Israel from the hand of the Egyptians that day.

EXODUS 14:23-30 NLT

God saved Israel on that day. Every year during the Passover season this event is celebrated so that the Jewish people never forget that they were once slaves. And more so that by God's mighty power, and His power alone, they were set free. But as we look back on this sequence of events—the process of how their freedom came to be—we discover that their freedom came not from passing through the Red Sea nor from the drowning of the Egyptian army. No! Instead, we find that their salvation came through their obedience.

This process actually began a couple of weeks before, on the night of what was to become known as Pesach (*pay´-sawk*), or Passover, a night on which every first born human and head of cattle in the country of Egypt was put to death at the hand of God's angel. Spared from this horror was every Israelite family that, in confidence that God was indeed going to kill every firstborn in the country, obediently sacrificed a lamb or goat earlier that evening, and spread some of its blood on their doorposts as they were commanded.

> *"On that same night I will pass through Egypt and strike down every firstborn of both people and animals, and I will bring judgment on all the gods of Egypt. I am the LORD. The blood will be a sign for you on the houses where you are, and when I see the blood, I will pass over you. No destructive plague will touch you when I strike Egypt."*
>
> EXODUS 12:13-14 NIV

In doing so, the angel of death had seen the blood and *passed over* those homes and spared the lives of the firstborn children living there, because God had already chosen the Israelites (when He long ago made a promise with Abraham, you may remember) to be His special possession.

And so through their obedience, like Noah and his family, God had already saved them. He had already determined to bring them out of Egypt, through the Red Sea, and lead them into the wilderness, and eventually into the Promised Land. Nothing the Israelites did or failed to do from then on was going to change what God was going to do. (If you don't believe me, keep reading through Exodus, Leviticus, Numbers and Deuteronomy, and you'll see they certainly tried!) For clearly, the plan God made had been set into motion millennia before, and it would take centuries more before it would find completion in Jesus.

In the meantime, the Israelites were to be a work-in-progress, and they were being made new. But the work that God would do within them, individually and as a nation, would take a lifetime to perfect. Their sanctification would take some time, even though God had already declared them to be holy. He had to, otherwise He could not dwell among them.

Imagine, before you can clean up some homeless man who hasn't had the chance to bathe or wash his clothes . . . ever, you have determined to stand in his presence and engage in a conversation with him. But you just can't tolerate it, so you have to do something that allows you to see (and smell) past his filthiness. You plug your nose and coerce him into a hot shower to bathe. You then spray him with musky cologne and dress him in clean clothes so you can now stand to be near him. Only then can you convince him to go with you to a place where you can help him on his road to recovery. But that is still only the beginning, because He still *thinks* like a homeless man. You may get him cleaned up, but he will want to keep his old clothes, "just in case." You tell him that you'll buy him new clothes, and he agrees—just as long as he gets to keep his old ones.

In the classic 1983 film *Trading Places*,[43] Eddie Murphy plays Billy Ray Valentine, a homeless beggar and thief living on the streets of New York. Caught up in a bet by two wealthy stockbrokers, Billy Ray is "taken" to a richly accommodated uptown apartment where he's told that there's no reason to steal anything, since everything within his reach has already been given to him. The apartment and everything in it now belong to Billy Ray, and they explain how he has been "chosen" to be groomed by them into a very successful stockbroker. He is being given a "new life," and he needs only to trust in the process of transformation.

But initially, Billy Ray can't contain himself. He finds great difficulty in believing his good fortune, and subversively attempts to steal everything of value he can find in the apartment, despite his hosts' urging. Of course, over the course of the film, Billy Ray really does change to become the very thing they told them he could be because of the proper influences, training and, most importantly, a change in the way he saw himself.

And that's the beauty of God (well, one of them). He chooses us first, then takes steps to make us acceptable, then spends the rest of our lives making us better, provided we go along with the program and trust the process.

---

43   *Trading Places.* Paramount Pictures (1983)

But you are a chosen people, a royal priesthood, a holy nation, a people for God's own possession, so that you may proclaim the praises of the One who called you out of darkness into His marvelous light. Once you were not a people, but now you are God's people. You were shown no mercy, but now you have been shown mercy.

1 PETER 2:9-10 TLV

THE SMITTEN ROCK

In another episode of their exodus, as the Israelites wandered through the wilderness, they had grown restless and concerned about their lack of water. They had been traveling for a while, and their water provisions were nearing critical levels, so they grew fearful.

There was no water for the people to drink at that place [called Kadesh in the Desert of Zin], so they rebelled against Moses and Aaron. The people blamed Moses and said, "If only we had died in the LORD's presence with our brothers! Why have you brought the congregation of the LORD's people into this wilderness to die, along with all our livestock? Why did you make us leave Egypt and bring us here to this terrible place? This land has no grain, no figs, no grapes, no pomegranates, and no water to drink!"

Moses and Aaron turned away from the people and went to the entrance of the Tabernacle, where they fell face down on the ground. Then the glorious presence of the LORD appeared to them, and the LORD said to Moses, "You and Aaron must take the staff and assemble the entire community. As the people watch, speak to the rock over there, and it will pour out its water. You will provide enough water from the rock to satisfy the whole community and their livestock."

So Moses took the staff from the LORD's presence, just as he commanded him. He and Aaron gathered the assembly

116

*together in front of the rock and Moses said to them, "Listen,
you rebels, must we bring you water out of this rock?" Then
Moses raised his arm and struck the rock twice with his staff.
Water gushed out, and the community and their livestock
drank.*

NUMBERS 20:2-11 NLT

Earlier in their travels (Exodus 17:6), Moses was in the same
situation when God instructed him to strike a rock to make
water flow. This time, though Moses is clearly directed to simply
speak to the rock to get the water moving, he instead *smote*[44] the
rock as he had once before, as if his skill with the staff was what
would cause the water to flow.

Sure, the water still poured out, but Moses got in big trouble
from God, and his punishment was to be kept from later entering
the Promised Land with his people.

*Then the LORD spoke to Moses and Aaron, "Because you did
not trust me enough to show me as holy before the Israelites,
therefore you will not bring this community into the land I
have given them."*

NUMBERS 20:12 NET

Interestingly, in our previous chapter we noted that the
Mishnah suggests that "smitten" waters are second only to
"living" waters for the purpose of ceremonial purification, and
to smite the water would be to strike it or cause a splash. This
indicates the potential for stirring up any standing water with a
stick or other device to get it circulating or agitated. This could
include a fountain (with a pump) or just a simple stirring with
the hand or foot. This is best represented in the story of the sick
man told in the gospel of John:

---

44 **nakah** (*naw-kaw´*)—*Hebrew,* meaning to strike or strike down. Strong's Number 5221
    Hebrew Concordance of the Old Testament. http://lexiconcordance.com/hebrew/4723.html

> *After [healing a boy in Galilee] there was a Jewish festival, and Jesus went up to Jerusalem. In Jerusalem near the Sheep Gate in the north city wall is a pool with the Aramaic name Bethsaida. It had five covered porches, and a crowd of people who were sick, blind, lame, and paralyzed sat there. A certain man was there who had been sick for thirty-eight years. When Jesus saw him lying there, knowing that he had already been there a long time, he asked him, "Do you want to get well?"*
>
> *The sick man answered him, "Sir, I don't have anyone who can put me in the water when it is stirred up. When I'm trying to get to it, someone else has gotten in ahead of me."*
>
> *Jesus said to him, "Get up! Pick up your mat and walk." Immediately the man was well, and he picked up his mat and walked. Now that day was the Sabbath.*
>
> JOHN 5:1-9 CEB

At this pool, at that time, it was believed that an angel would come down periodically[45] to stir the water, giving the water, for a short time afterwards, healing properties. While the effectiveness of this pool's healing powers was only legend, there must have been at least one individual historically who had seemed to find healing there for such a belief to persist. And after the healing by Jesus of this particular young man that day, I'm sure the legendary properties of the pool grew quite notably.

But here we notice that Jesus didn't use the water of the pool to heal the man. Jesus didn't tell him to get back into the water. Nope, He simply asked the man if he'd like the obstacles to his faith removed. And once that was done, Jesus invited the man to get up and walk. Whether the man chose to follow Jesus or not was up to him. But at least now the man had no excuse.

---

45   A handful of early Greek manuscripts include this addition to verse 3: *[waiting for the moving of the water. For an angel of the Lord went down and stirred up the water at certain times. Whoever first stepped in after the stirring of the water was healed from whatever disease which he suffered]*. However, most textual scholars do not accept its authenticity because the earliest and best manuscripts exclude it. As a result, most modern translations omit it.

Anyway, water that was in motion clearly had a purifying, if not healing, power. For every prescription, fresh water from a variety of sources was needed to bring cleansing and transformation—physically, emotionally, and spiritually. But what is extremely evident is that the water itself is only part of the process.

The water doesn't bring about the change, it only facilitates it.

Where Have Those Feet Been?
Chapter 11: Dirty Little Things

FOOT WASHING WAS A VERY COMMON PRACTICE in ancient times, since all roadways were generally regular old dusty dirt . . . with an added feature. Folks all wore sandals of some fashion, but those nearly bare feet, combined with often hours of travel, resulted in quite filthy feet indeed.

Keep in mind, of course, in those days people weren't driving Toyotas, Fords, Chevys or Subarus, replete with their toxic emissions. No, they were driving camels, cattle, oxen, sheep, donkeys and goats, replete with *their* toxic emissions! Such transportation and walking cargo didn't "hold it" until the next gas station. The animals relieved themselves as they moved, which was on the very highway on which everyone else was traveling.

This means that those designer sandals did nothing but keep stones from piercing the soles of their wearers' feet, failing to protect them from the literal filth on the ground. While the sandals would keep such stuff from squishing through their toes (nice and steamy in the early morning), it didn't keep it off their feet.

So when people came to their own or another's abode, how did they keep such junk from being transplanted into their home? Well, typically, they'd simply remove their shoes and wash their own feet as they stepped inside (just as we may remove our shoes at the door and leave them in the entryway). But if there were household servants present, then they would be tasked with the job of washing the enterer's feet. If you were lucky, the same servant that was awarded that responsibility could then get up and go prepare a meal. And this courtesy extended to any visitor of the home, whether strange or familiar, for it was important that the filth of the world not contaminate their dwelling place.

We must also realize that the opportunity to take a daily bath was not an option (and still isn't in some places) where there was no running (or living) water. Washing was a luxury, and was therefore, for most, not something done as frequently as desired.[46]

Understanding this, one can more readily see the significance of Jesus' act of washing the disciples' feet following the Last Supper.

> *[Jesus] got up from the meal, removed his outer clothes, took a towel and tied it around himself. He poured water into the washbasin and began to wash the disciples' feet and to dry them with the towel he had wrapped around himself.*
>
> *Then he came to Simon Peter. Peter said to him, "Lord, are you going to wash my feet?"*
>
> *Jesus replied, "You do not understand what I am doing now, but you will understand after these things …"*
>
> *Simon Peter said to him, "Lord, wash not only my feet, but also my hands and my head!"*
>
> *Jesus replied, "The one who has bathed needs only to wash his feet, but is completely clean …"*
>
> *When he had finished washing their feet, he put on his clothes and returned to his place. "Do you understand what I have done for you?" he asked them. "You call me 'Teacher' and*

---

46 Only after the advent and availability of running water in the earlier part of the 1800s did people begin bathing more frequently, and then only in urban areas by the wealthy. In biblical times, bathing occurred only occasionally as needed. Following the bubonic plague in the fourteenth century, many believed that dirt on the skin prevented the transmission of disease. So most folks bathed infrequently, as few as three or four times a year! Today, in Western cultures, the average person bathes or showers daily, with many doing so as often as two or three times a day.

'Lord,' and rightly so, for that is what I am. Now that I, your Lord and Teacher, have washed your feet, you also should wash one another's feet. I have set you an example that you should do as I have done for you. Very truly I tell you, no servant is greater than his master, nor is a messenger greater than the one who sent him."
JOHN 13:4-16 NET

The disciples were dumbfounded. This was just not something someone of Jesus' stature should do. Touching another's feet was a very lowly thing to do and washing them was all the more so.

Jesus' cousin John, the Baptizer (that wasn't his real name), understood the significance of touching feet when he said,

"After me comes One who is mightier than I am," he proclaimed. "I'm not worthy to stoop down and untie the strap of His sandals!"
MARK 1:7 TLV

John was saying that he was even lower on the totem pole than a servant when it came to Jesus. (That's an ironic expression, though, as totem poles in many cultures render the "greatest" imagery closest to the ground.) So, Jesus removing His suit and tie and washing His friends' feet, as would a slave, was indeed a shocking example of servant leadership. Here was Jesus, the son of the Most High, serving as the most low. (I'm being figurative, of course. As a carpenter, Jesus was a blue-collar worker who likely never wore a suit.)

Was Jesus instructing all of us to follow His example and likewise practice the washing of one another's feet? I don't think so, really, since that was very much a cultural act. But it's quite fascinating to me that this did not become a lasting sacrament in the Church, as did communion and baptism (as we're discussing), even though it seems that Jesus was very explicit about us doing so. I quote again:

> *"Now that I, your Lord and Teacher, have washed your feet, you also should wash one another's feet. I have set you an example that you should do as I have done for you."*
> JOHN 13:14-15 NET

But I (like everyone else) do believe that He's simply providing a figurative example of servant leadership; that we must position ourselves as servants when leading. For when we lead, we must clearly demonstrate that our position is one of service. Whether we are leading our spouse, our family, our church, our community, or our nation, we are serving them as that leader. But you know this already. The last time we spoke of this foot-washing event,[47] we noted that Jesus was responding to an argument the disciples were having about who was greatest among them (Luke 22:24-27).

Anyway, having now examined what foot-washing was all about, we can plainly see that this has absolutely nothing to do with our discussion of baptism, and so we can dismiss this topic entirely.

IT WAS ONLY THE LAW

Okay. So do you remember a while back when I said that foot-washing didn't have anything to do with baptism? Well, I was wondering if perhaps there was a connection there after all . . .

During the *Original Detox Program*, we looked at the thirtieth chapter of Exodus and discovered that the priests were instructed to wash their hands and feet before entering the Tent of Meeting. There was also a special oil that was to be manufactured and used to anoint the priests to mark them as holy and fit for service in the house of the Lord. But they were also to be physically clean

---

47   Another shameless yet relevant reference to my previous work, *The First Communion: The Making of the Last Supper* (June 2022).

before they could be considered ceremonially clean.

Dirty feet were a big deal. God didn't want His servants leaving road remnants in His House, so He made sure they kept things sanitary. But this all came down to a matter of worship and respect. God demanded that the people treat Him with reverence and respect, not because He was full of Himself, but **it was important that the people learned how to separate the world from their worship.**

If they could each just "come as you are", they would. They wouldn't stop to even consider how marvelous God was, and how special their relationship with Him could be. If they could be allowed to just wander on into the sanctuary with all of the filth the world brought with it, they would never be able to separate themselves spiritually from that world. (Hmm, now I'm wondering about the way I dress for church.)

God was setting them up for success by teaching them how to behave differently from that world; and that to make their relationship with Him "special" would demand some special effort, attention, and sacrifice. If they were going to be His children, they were going to have to be recognizable as such, and this meant being special in every way, shape, and form.

As Christians, we frequently miss the point of being set apart by God. We don't often see our relationship with Him as being notable because we mostly do our own thing, worrying about our own lives and circumstances, ignorant of the truth that our day-to-day struggles are not our purpose. We have been chosen for something meaningful, and running around with our heads cut off, worrying about our job and our next meal is not that "meaningful something."

And if we do not set ourselves apart for God, how can He set us apart and use us for His purpose? Not that we must acquire any special skill or quality (we already have them), but we must set our hearts apart for His use, being willing to let Him do good works within us.

> *Now in a wealthy home there are not only gold and silver vessels, but also ones made of wood and of clay, and some are for honorable use, but others for ignoble use. So if someone cleanses himself of such behavior, he will be a vessel for honorable use, set apart, useful for the Master, prepared for every good work. But keep away from youthful passions, and pursue righteousness, faithfulness, love, and peace, in company with others who call on the Lord from a pure heart.*
>
> 2 Timothy 2:20-22 NET

But if we continue to live our lives as though we were just ordinary people trapped in ordinary lives destined to do ordinary things, then are we really believers? Can Jesus truly consider us His disciples if we're only claiming association with Him by name, and not by faith or action? Remember, if we are not living by Jesus' words, then we are living against them!

> *"On judgment day many will say to me, 'Lord! Lord! We prophesied in your name and cast out demons in your name and performed many miracles in your name.' But I will reply, 'I never knew you. Get away from me, you who break God's laws.'"*
>
> Matthew 7:22-23 NLT

> *So we are lying if we say we have fellowship with God but go on living in spiritual darkness; we are not practicing the truth. If we claim we have no sin, we are only fooling ourselves and not living in the truth. If we claim we have not sinned, we are calling God a liar and showing that his word has no place in our hearts.*
>
> 1 John 1:6, 8, 10 NLT

SWEET FEET

And so, even though dirty feet were a big issue, it was still an everyday concern that affected everyone, except for royalty who had the benefit of horses, chariots and carriages (and servants backs) to keep their feet off the ground. For the rest of society, however, it would seem they all had pretty stinky feet. But Mary, the sister of Lazarus and Martha, close friends of Jesus, made quite a spectacle of herself:

> *Six days before Passover, Jesus came to Bethany, home of Lazarus, whom Jesus had raised from the dead. Lazarus and his sisters hosted a dinner for him. Martha served and Lazarus was among those who joined him at the table. Then Mary took an extraordinary amount, almost three-quarters of a pound, of very expensive perfume made of pure nard. She anointed Jesus' feet with it, then wiped his feet dry with her hair. The house was filled with the aroma of the perfume.*
>
> *Judas Iscariot, one of his disciples (the one who was about to betray him), complained, "This perfume was worth a year's wages! Why wasn't it sold and the money given to the poor?" (He said this not because he cared about the poor but because he was a thief. He carried the money bag and would take what was in it.)*
>
> *Then Jesus said, "Leave her alone. This perfume was to be used in preparation for my burial, and this is how she has used it. You will always have the poor among you, but you won't always have me."*
>
> JOHN 12:1-8 CEB

Because of the way people reclined on the floor or on a couch with a table in their midst, their feet were quite exposed to those who served the food at such an event. As a result, it was quite easy for Mary, in this episode, to position herself at Jesus' feet to anoint him with her tears and perfume. (The versions of this event in the other gospels convey varying details, but all with equal results, even though they are often misunderstood as being unique and separate events.)

But here she is, holding and kissing Jesus' feet! Of course, these are the cleanest and sweetest smelling feet ever, and perhaps the perfume just made them that much sweeter.[48] And while the feet were the lowliest and dirtiest part of a person, Mary was quite content to humble herself for the sake of her Lord.

---

48   *God's feet* most certainly touched the ground, and Jesus' were likely as dirty as those of Lazarus reclining next to him. Read *Three Places God's Feet Touched the Ground*, Adriel Sanchez (October 2020). https://corechristianity.com/resource-library/articles/three-places-gods-feet-touched-the-ground/

A Bird Bath

Chapter 12: Getting Wet With a Purpose

*Then Jesus came from Galilee to the Jordan to be baptized by
John. But John tried to deter him, saying, "I need to be baptized
by you, and do you come to me?" Jesus replied, "Let it be so
now; it is proper for us to do this to fulfill all righteousness."
Then John consented. As soon as Jesus was baptized, he went
up out of the water. At that moment heaven was opened, and
he saw the Spirit of God descending like a dove and alighting
on him. And a voice from heaven said, "This is my Son, whom I
love; with him I am well pleased."*

MATTHEW 3:13-17 NIV

JOHN, SON OF ZECHARIAH, was commonly known as "Creepy
John" to the locals.[49] He had moved out of his parents' home
as a young man and headed out to live in the wilderness until
such time as he was called by God to begin his public ministry.
Up until then, he lived a "homeless" life as a hermit consuming
primarily honey and locusts (when they were in season), all the
while managing to abstain from all forms of alcohol, simply
because his dad told him God said not to (Luke 1:15).

---

49   *The Chosen (TV Series)*. Directed, produced and co-written by Dallas Jenkins. The nickname
"Creepy John" is a creative liberty of the show's writers and does not appear in Scripture.
The moniker "John the Baptist" actually appears only twice in most English translations, in
Mark 1:4 and in Matthew 3:1. In John's gospel, the author refers to John son of Zechariah
simply as "John."

Then, one day:

> *During the high priesthood of Annas and Caiaphas, the word of God came upon John, the son of Zechariah, in the wilderness. And he came into all the surrounding region of the Jordan, proclaiming an immersion of repentance for the removal of sins.*
>
> Luke 3:2-3 TLV

For what was likely several weeks before Jesus' appearance, John preached a baptism of repentance. As we now know, baptism was already familiar to the Jewish communities. Its purpose up to that point, however, was a bit different. Earlier we discussed how, in addition to the priests, everyone at some point or another was required to undergo ceremonial washing by water to remove their uncleanness. Even converts to Judaism were required to undergo ceremonial water immersion to purify themselves.

But remember, *baptisma* is a Greek term, not a Hebrew one. Since the English language had yet to be developed in the greater Roman Empire, one of the most common languages of the day was Greek. So when the New Testament authors wrote of "baptism" they were simply using the Greek term that meant to be immersed (or overwhelmed). Jews today may even object to the use of the word baptism in conjunction with any Jewish practice, simply because it is not a Hebrew term, and it's considered by them to be an exclusively Christian invention.

But the word itself has such a simple meaning and, at the time of its addition to the Greek language, had nothing to do with the Christian practice that did not yet exist. This is demonstrated plainly by the fact that John is baptizing people for quite some time before Jesus even shows up on the scene. Baptism, then, had no specific religious connotation, and only described a technique for getting people "wet with a purpose."

LIKE A DOVE

Are you aware that none of the gospel writers actually saw the Holy Spirit descend on Jesus? Nor do any of them claim they physically saw a dove at the time of Jesus' baptism. Instead, we discover they are each only recording John the Baptizer's testimony, not their own.

> *Then John testified, "I saw the Holy Spirit descending like a dove from heaven and resting upon him. I didn't know he was the one, but when God sent me to baptize with water, he told me, 'The one on whom you see the Spirit descend and rest is the one who will baptize with the Holy Spirit.' I saw this happen to Jesus, so I testify that he is the Chosen One of God."*
> JOHN 1:32-34 NLT

> *As soon as Jesus was baptized, he went up out of the water. At that moment heaven was opened, and [John the Baptizer] saw the Spirit of God descending like a dove and alighting on him.*
> MATTHEW 3:16 NIV

"Like a dove" is John's way of communicating what he perceived. The Holy Spirit became visible to John from somewhere above Jesus and seems to have had the appearance of something that was bright white and could carry itself through the air as might a bird. He testified that it was not a dove but rather *like a dove* in its appearance and actions. Surely John had never seen the Holy Spirit before, so how else might he describe Him?

So God sent John to baptize with water, to immerse everyone who recognized that they were not right with God and believed his message of repentance—to prepare their hearts for the coming of the Messiah (or *Greek*, Christ), Jesus.

John preached that he immersed the penitent with water, but that someone was coming who would immerse them in the Holy Spirit. But only those with a broken heart would be positioned to receive Him.

Now Scripture only gives us brief excerpts regarding John's messaging, but his teaching was clearly that of expressing one's need for change, a change that can only come in the aftermath of sorrow or remorse.

The New Testament writers used the Greek word *metanoia* to refer to repentance. *Metanoia* means a change of mind, thought, or thinking so powerful that it changes one's very way of living. In Hebrew, this concept is familiar as well. In her article, *What Did Jesus Mean by Repent? The Hebrew Meaning of Teshuva*, Estera Wieja explains,[50]

> The Hebrew word we translate as "repentance" is *teshuva* (*těh-shoo´-vah*). And teshuva is a lot more than a feeling of guilt or regret. In fact, it derives from the verb "to return"! It is not just adjusting the course, but completely turning back around—physically, emotionally and spiritually. Teshuva is more than just stopping a certain behavior, being sorry or apologizing one time. This is a continuous decision to return to God and to receive a new beginning. In Jewish thought, the purpose of repentance is to go through a transformation. It is not just an apologetic confession.

With this we should understand that as John preached a "baptism of repentance for the forgiveness of sins" (Mark 1:4), folks lined up to be baptized because they understood that, while they each felt they obeyed the law (were good people) and offered the required sacrifices regularly, they hadn't yet turned their hearts back to God.

Now, as they each awaited their turn by the river, **they had**

---

50 *What Did Jesus Mean by Repent? The Hebrew Meaning of Teshuva.* Estera Wieja (August 2021). https://firmisrael.org/learn/what-did-jesus-mean-by-repent-the-hebrew-meaning-of-teshuva/

already made their decision to change their lives and go God's way. Even those who were still standing in line when The Baptizer was arrested by Herod (see Mark 6), and who missed their chance to get baptized by John, had already repented and turned to God. They were ready. They were ready to receive Jesus when that time came.

But why did Jesus get baptized? Surely, He was without sin and needed no repentance or forgiveness, and to suggest otherwise would certainly be blasphemy! But perhaps we can understand that John's baptism was intended to fall short. Because repentance is necessary to position our hearts to receive forgiveness through the death, burial and resurrection of Jesus Christ, John's baptism alone couldn't accomplish that because Jesus had yet to be glorified. What John's baptism was meant to accomplish would and could only be fulfilled in Jesus. As Mike Winger explains:[51]

> "Jesus is stepping into the symbolism of His own atoning death and victorious resurrection. Because He comes to fulfill the meaning of baptism—in fact, to give it meaning. Your baptism matters because Jesus fulfilled it and accomplished it on the cross."

WATER & SPIRIT

Jesus [said], "I tell you the truth, unless you are born again, you cannot see the Kingdom of God."

"What do you mean?" exclaimed Nicodemus. "How can an old man go back into his mother's womb and be born again?"

Jesus replied, "I assure you, no one can enter the Kingdom of God without being born of water and the Spirit. Humans can reproduce only human life, but the Holy Spirit gives birth to spiritual life. So don't be surprised when I say, 'You must be born again.' The wind blows wherever it wants. Just as you can hear the wind but can't tell where it comes from or where it is

---

51   *Why Baptize Jesus?* Mike Winger (May 2019). https://youtu.be/l1uNs8XW9JE?t=774

Some have taught that "being born of water and the Spirit" is decisive evidence that one must be "born of water" (baptized) to be saved. But Jesus does not separate the entities of water and Spirit into two. Here He combines them.

Jesus was speaking in private to a man named Nicodemus who was a Pharisee—a member of the Jewish ruling council—who was not only familiar with Old Testament law and procedures but who was also a renowned rabbi of the same. On this particular evening, he and Jesus were having a one-on-one conversation, and Nicodemus was already very open to the possibility that Jesus was who He claimed to be, because Nicodemus had been quite aware of—if not a witness to—many of the things Jesus was saying and doing publicly up to that point.

So, Jesus didn't need to be secretive or ambiguous with His words here. Nicodemus knew what baptism was, as the Jews already practiced immersion into water for the variety of reasons we've already discussed. If Jesus meant "baptize" when He said "born of water" He would have just said so. This is also why, after saying "water and the Spirit," Jesus doesn't mention water again in this conversation.

Instead we discover that Jesus is pairing the two terms "water and Spirit" as one, indicating that they are not two separate and distinct things but rather one thing of which Nicodemus would most certainly be familiar. Because in the Old Testament, both water and Spirit regularly referred to spiritual renewal and cleansing.

The palace and the city will be deserted, and busy towns will be empty. Wild donkeys will frolic and flocks will graze in the empty forts and watchtowers until at last the Spirit is poured out on us from heaven. Then the wilderness will become a fertile field, and the fertile field will yield bountiful crops.

Isaiah 32:14-15 NLT

God regularly used the language of water to symbolize the Holy Spirit. Oftentimes, God literally used water to demonstrate the power of the Holy Spirit. But here, even though Nicodemus understands the correlation between the two, he can still barely grasp what Jesus is telling him: that he "must be born again" by the living water of the Holy Spirit.

A Samaritan woman came to the well [in Samaria] to draw water. Jesus said to her, "Give me some water to drink." His disciples had gone into the city to buy him some food.

The Samaritan woman asked, "Why do you, a Jewish man, ask for something to drink from me, a Samaritan woman?" (Jews and Samaritans didn't associate with each other.)

Jesus responded, "If you recognized God's gift and who is saying to you, 'Give me some water to drink,' you would be asking him and he would give you living water."

The woman said to him, "Sir, you don't have a bucket and the well is deep. Where would you get this living water? You aren't greater than our father Jacob, are you? He gave this well to us, and he drank from it himself, as did his sons and his livestock."

Jesus answered, "Everyone who drinks this water will be thirsty again, but whoever drinks from the water that I will give will never be thirsty again. The water that I give will become in those who drink it a spring of water that bubbles up into eternal life."

John 4:7-14 CEB

In this exchange, Jesus equates this *living water* with the Holy Spirit, and how being filled by His Spirit quenches one's spiritual thirst. He explains to the woman that what she thirsts for is something that only He can quench. Only the Holy Spirit—this Living Water—can transform her soul into its own well-spring that could, not only forever satisfy her own spirit but, bubble over into the lives of those around her. In fact, we find that when we drink in this Living Water, it spills over uncontrollably. It becomes uncontainable, a torrential outpouring of exhilaration and refreshment. And indeed, this is exactly what happens:

> *The woman put down her water jar and went into the city. She said to the people, "Come and see a man who has told me everything I've done! Could this man be the Christ?" They left the city and were on their way to see Jesus. Many Samaritans in that city believed in Jesus because of the woman's word when she testified, "He told me everything I've ever done."*
>
> *So when the Samaritans came to Jesus, they asked him to stay with them, and he stayed there two days. Many more believed because of his word, and they said to the woman, "We no longer believe because of what you said, for we have heard for ourselves and know that this one is truly the savior of the world."*
>
> JOHN 4:28-30, 39-42 CEB

To "drink in" something means to "take in" or "bask in" something, usually an experience of some kind, such as *drinking in the sunrise.* In this instance, drinking in the living water of the Spirit would mean to take in, absorb, and make Him part of us. But how does one accomplish this? Can we simply take Him captive at some point, in some way, and force Him to reside within us? How exactly do we get our hands on this Living Water? Under what circumstances can we receive the Holy Spirit?

Moreover, is the Holy Spirit necessary for our salvation? As we'll see next, the New Testament shows varying examples of conversion, some that involve the Spirit and some that don't.

Come, Spirit, Come!
Chapter 13: Indwellable Markings

*Now the earth was formless and empty, darkness was over the
surface of the deep, and the Spirit of God was hovering over
the waters.*

Genesis 1:2 NIV

THE TERM "SPIRIT OF GOD" is mentioned nearly a dozen times in
the Old Testament (only in English translations, of course), and
the roles of the Holy Spirit in the Old Testament mostly revolve
around the expression of God's presence or power.

In the New Testament, this doesn't change. Every manifestation
of the Holy Spirit represents God's presence moving through and
among believers. And as we see below, His presence can often
impact those who do not yet believe.

Jesus moved in the Spirit as the power of God to heal and
reveal God in the world. God's Spirit was not only powerful but
would eventually be extremely personal. The Holy Spirit would
soon live inside each believer, leading and giving them the words
to say in challenging circumstances, teaching and reminding
them of the words of Jesus, counseling and helping them to live
new lives with new purpose.

GO TELL IT ON THE MOUNTAIN

So, when exactly can one expect to receive the gift of the Holy
Spirit? Does He come at the moment of conversion, at the instant

of accepting Jesus as Lord? As we look more closely at what the Bible tells us, we'll need to evaluate what happens both in the gospel accounts and in the New Testament book of Acts.

> *Then the eleven disciples left for Galilee, going to the mountain where Jesus had told them to go. When they saw him, they worshiped him—but some of them doubted! Jesus came and told his disciples, "I have been given all authority in heaven and on earth. Therefore, go and make disciples of all the nations, baptizing them in the name of the Father and the Son and the Holy Spirit. Teach these new disciples to obey all the commands I have given you. And be sure of this: I am with you always, even to the end of the age."*
>
> MATTHEW 28:16-20 NLT

Jesus commanded His disciples to travel throughout the "world" and share the gospel so that all people everywhere could eventually hear and receive the Good News. But this direction was given the last day He walked the earth. Up to that time, there are no recorded conversions that took place after Resurrection Sunday. And so those baptisms that occurred earlier, those performed by John as well as those performed by Jesus' disciples (John 4:1-2), would have been incomplete, as we've discussed.

Only now, after the Resurrection, did those baptisms find fulfillment. But because Jesus was still hanging around (or was that Judas? . . . *Too soon?*), God had not yet sent the Holy Spirit to indwell the believers. Instead, Jesus tells His followers that the Holy Spirit is not a separate entity, but rather an additional expression of the Trinity who would soon come:

> *"If you love me, keep my commands. And I will ask the Father, and he will give you another advocate to help you and be with you forever—the Spirit of truth. The world cannot accept him, because it neither sees him nor knows him. But you know him,*

for he lives with you and will be in you."
JOHN 14:15-17 NIV

Jesus says, "He lives with you" and then again that He "will be in you." Which is it? Because Jesus is Himself an expression of the Trinity, He was present with them there. But later, at a time when Jesus would no longer be on the earth, He would be *in them* as the Holy Spirit. Connecting this together with what we've learned previously, none of His disciples had yet to be "born again" since they had not been reborn through His Spirit, which was still to come. They were "believers" but they had not yet received the indwelling of the Spirit.

On the last day, the climax of the festival, Jesus stood and shouted to the crowds, "Anyone who is thirsty may come to me! Anyone who believes in me may come and drink! For the Scriptures declare, 'Rivers of living water will flow from his heart.'" (When he said "living water," he was speaking of the Spirit, who would be given to everyone believing in him. But the Spirit had not yet been given, because Jesus had not yet entered into his glory.)
JOHN 7:37-39 NLT

But when they came to Jesus and found that he was already dead, they did not break his legs. Instead, one of the soldiers pierced Jesus' side with a spear, bringing a sudden flow of blood and water.
JOHN 19:33-34 NIV

But back on the evening of the Resurrection, Jesus had appeared to many of them and:

Again he said, "Peace be with you. As the Father has sent me, so I am sending you." Then he breathed on them and said,

"Receive the Holy Spirit."
John 20:22 NLT

At that time He bestowed on those present the gift of the Holy Spirit, though still not yet an indwelling. He was imbuing them with temporary power because He was again "sending them out." They were not yet born again of Living Water, and their lives were not yet truly transformed, though that time was coming soon, as we'll see.

Putting these pieces together, it becomes clear that water baptism and the receiving of the Holy Spirit were not synonymous as long as Jesus walked the earth. Only after He was glorified was the Holy Spirit a gift to be received.

When you believed, you were marked in him with a seal, the promised Holy Spirit, who is a deposit guaranteeing our inheritance until the redemption of those who are God's possession–to the praise of his glory.
Ephesians 1:13-14 NIV

AMBER WAVES OF GRAIN

According to the Old Testament book of Leviticus, the first Sunday following Passover (which turned out to be Resurrection Sunday in this particular year) was known as *First Fruits*, the beginning of a seven-week festival called The Festival of Weeks:

Then the Lord spoke to Moses, saying, "Speak to the sons of Israel and say to them, 'When you enter the land which I am going to give to you and you gather its harvest, then you shall bring in the sheaf of the first fruits of your harvest to the priest. He shall wave the sheaf before the Lord for you to be accepted; on the day after the Sabbath the priest shall wave it.'"
Leviticus 23:9-11 NASB

The Gospels tell us that Jesus did not continue walking daily with His disciples after the Resurrection as He had done prior, but they do tell us He made regular "appearances" over the forty days that followed. While most of His disciples had each returned to their own daily routines at that point—while continuing to do life together—they just went about their regular days (which were anything but regular) trying to figure out exactly what they were supposed to do now that Jesus wasn't hanging out with them all the time, while simultaneously awaiting their very next encounter with Him.

But on the fortieth day, Jesus meets with them for the last time, communicating the directives Matthew shared with us earlier (Matthew 28:16-20). And then, as Luke tells us, Jesus says this:

> *"And now I will send the Holy Spirit, just as my Father promised. But stay here in the city until the Holy Spirit comes and fills you with power from heaven." Then Jesus led them to Bethany, and lifting his hands to heaven, he blessed them. While he was blessing them, he left them and was taken up to heaven. So they worshiped him and then returned to Jerusalem filled with great joy. And they spent all of their time in the Temple, praising God.*
>
> LUKE 24:49-53 CEB

Jesus left the earth to return to His Father's side and left the apostles and those with them instructions to continue waiting indefinitely. Of course, they had no idea what to expect, only that Jesus promised the Spirit would come and fill them with the power of heaven.

Now it turns out that fifty days after that initial day of "waving" comes the second *First Fruits* offering that marks the beginning of the grain harvest. This feast was known later by the Gentile believers as *Pentecost*, deriving its name from the Greek word for fiftieth.

> *"'From the day after the Sabbath, the day you brought the
> sheaf of the wave offering, count off seven full weeks. Count
> off fifty days up to the day after the seventh Sabbath, and then
> present an offering of new grain to the LORD.'"*
>
> LEVITICUS 23:15-16 NIV

And when that fiftieth day came, just ten days after Jesus'
ascension, we learn:

> *When the day of Pentecost came, [the disciples] were all
> together in one place. Suddenly a sound like the blowing of
> a violent wind came from heaven and filled the whole house
> where they were sitting. They saw what seemed to be tongues
> of fire that separated and came to rest on each of them. All of
> them were filled with the Holy Spirit and began to speak in
> other languages as the Spirit enabled them.*
>
> *Now there were staying in Jerusalem God-fearing Jews
> from every nation under heaven. When they heard this sound,
> a crowd came together in bewilderment, because each one
> heard their own language being spoken. Utterly amazed, they
> asked: "Aren't all these who are speaking Galileans? Then how
> is it that each of us hears them in our native language? ...*
>
> *We hear them speaking in our own languages about the
> great deeds God has done!" All were astounded and greatly
> confused, saying to one another, "What does this mean?"*
>
> *Some, however, made fun of them and said, "They have
> had too much wine."*
>
> ACTS 2:5-8, 11-13 NIV

There were at least eleven apostles who were now *immersed* in
the Holy Spirit and spoke in these foreign languages (tongues),
and perhaps as many as one hundred twenty other disciples were
there too (see Acts 1:15).

Now, it's often interpreted from the text that the disciples
explicitly spoke different languages out loud, as it says, "all of

them . . . began to speak in other languages *as the Spirit enabled them.*" But, examining the hearers' response, "How is it that each of us hears them in our own language," it seems more reasonable that the disciples were actually speaking with the voice of the Holy Spirit, in unity, through which those present individually *perceived* the message in their own language.

I suggest this only because if there were eleven (or one hundred thirty) men shouting the Word of God into an open area of at least thirty-thousand square feet—in different languages at the same time—the message would have been wildly incoherent. It would have been exceedingly difficult for the voice of so many to have otherwise successfully penetrated the ears and hearts of so many people present in that space.

But because God is a god of order, it seems plausible that the disciples all spoke with the same voice, as it was in fact the Holy Spirit that moved throughout the crowd, "piercing even to the point of dividing soul from spirit, and joints from marrow; judging the desires and thoughts of the heart" (Hebrews 4:12-13 NET).

But to those present who were not open to receiving the Spirit's interpretation, it would have all sounded like gibberish, as they mocked, "They have had too much wine." As it is written:

> *For the message of the cross is foolishness to those who are perishing, but to us who are being saved it is the power of God.*
>
> 1 CORINTHIANS 1:18 NIV

Through the Holy Spirit, God used the disciples to share the Good News with thousands of men from all nations right there in a single gathering. Then, in the same way, Peter began to speak as a single voice, and yet a large percentage of the men present from "every nation" were still able to hear the Word of God spoken, with a response that resulted in their acceptance of that message and an immediate response of baptism of over three thousand new believers that day.

> *When the people heard this, they were cut to the heart and said to Peter and the other apostles, "Brothers, what shall we do?"*
>
> *Peter replied, "Repent and be baptized, every one of you, in the name of Jesus Christ for the forgiveness of your sins. And you will receive the gift of the Holy Spirit. The promise is for you and your children and for all who are far off–for all whom the Lord our God will call."*
>
> *With many other words he warned them; and he pleaded with them, "Save yourselves from this corrupt generation." Those who accepted his message were baptized, and about three thousand were added to their number that day.*
>
> Acts 2:37-39 NIV

So it seems that these 3,000 were indeed the beginning of the new grain offering God was expecting (Leviticus 23:15-16). Talk about a First Harvest!

WHAT SHALL WE DO?

Prior to His crucifixion Jesus announced simply, "Repent, for the kingdom of heaven is near." But now, on the day of Pentecost, Peter's message is "repent and be baptized," since the kingdom of God was now "in their midst" (Luke 17:20-21).

Peter said that in receipt for their repentance and baptism they would receive the gift of the Holy Spirit. But it's here we might see a two-step process. One, they accepted the gospel message by recognizing Jesus' sacrifice for them (*Brothers, what shall we do?*). And two, they demonstrated repentance by making the decision to live differently, to turn back towards God and live His way instead of their own. This repentance was then confirmed by their baptism.

But that wasn't all. They were also about to receive a new Counselor who would walk with them on their new paths,

146

teaching them from within, and making the changes in them that would pour out onto the lives of others and change the world.

But would they receive the Holy Spirit as a result of their baptism or as a result of their earlier acceptance and repentance? It must have taken a long while to baptize three thousand people! Did the guy at the end of the line have to wait for his portion of the Holy Spirit until he came up out of the water?

We've established that the term baptism, as it is translated to us from the Greek, means to immerse, typically in water. But Jesus had told His disciples to wait in Jerusalem because "John baptized with water, but in a few days you will be [immersed in] the Holy Spirit" (Acts 1:5). He then explained that they would receive power when the Holy Spirit came upon them at that time. So, in this use of "baptize" Jesus is clearly distinguishing between the waters of baptism and the outpouring of the Holy Spirit on Pentecost.

This outpouring, as we've seen, was not an indwelling of the Spirit to all those present, but rather a stirring or moving of the Spirit for the purpose of stimulating change and communicating His presence. This is amplified by Peter's own response to the people when he said, "Repent and be baptized . . . and you will receive the gift of the Holy Spirit."

In this circumstance, those present did not receive the Holy Spirit at the moment of their hearing of Peter's message. That's because simply acknowledging one's sin and failures is not enough. And just admitting that you "need Jesus" is not enough. Criminals plead guilty all the time. And those convicted regularly appeal to a higher court. So just admitting that "I am a sinner" is not enough.

Instead, the apostle Paul details for us the two steps mentioned earlier:

> *If you declare with your mouth, "Jesus is Lord," and believe in your heart that God raised him from the dead, you will be saved. For it is with your heart that you believe and are*

> *justified, and it is with your mouth that you profess your faith and are saved. As Scripture says, "Anyone who believes in him will never be put to shame." For there is no difference between Jew and Gentile—the same Lord is Lord of all and richly blesses all who call on him, for, "Everyone who calls on the name of the Lord will be saved."*
>
> Romans 10:9-13 NIV

These two parts seem to go hand in hand: "belief" and "confession" (from Latin *confessus*, meaning to declare or acknowledge). The first part, belief or faith, comes in the form of accepting the truth of the gospel message that Jesus paid the price for our sin—our failure to live up to God's glorious standard—and that through His death, burial, and resurrection, we can live out our justification before God.

The second part is the declaration, or confession, that Jesus is Lord, which can only come from the place of repentance, so that one is positioned to receive Him.

> *Therefore I want you to know that no one who is speaking by the Spirit of God says, "Jesus be cursed," and no one can say, "Jesus is Lord," except by the Holy Spirit.*
>
> 1 Corinthians 12:3 NIV

Such a confession is swearing one's loyalty to His kingdom and accepting the rights and privileges that members of His kingdom enjoy, while simultaneously accepting the responsibilities and way of living to which all subjects of His kingdom are expected to abide. This confession that must be "declared," and water baptism seems to participate in the role of this second part.

It's important to note, in the very statement Paul makes above, baptism is not mentioned. For he is writing to believers with the assumption that they *have* been baptized. But the omission of baptism here also appears to be an indicator that it is *not* a requirement for salvation.

You'll remember the value of being a part of a good kingdom, and that the process of pledging fealty to a king must be, by definition, a formal or public act.[52]

As many men and women in our current culture avoid the commitment of marriage by forgoing any formally recognized ceremony, neither can they claim to be "married" simply because they live together and wear wedding bands. For if marriage could be accomplished without a formal ceremony—even at a courthouse or a chapel in Las Vegas—then why is there such a reluctance to participate in a ceremony to make it official?

Like most legal transactions, the wedding ceremony involves at least two *witnesses*. And this has basis found in the Bible, of course:

> *"One witness is not enough to convict anyone accused of any crime or offense they may have committed. A matter must be established by the testimony of two or three witnesses."*
> DEUTERONOMY 19:15 NIV

So, while I'm not suggesting that marriage is a crime (though possibly offensive), witnesses must be present to establish its legitimacy. Likewise, baptism must have witnesses, else there's no value in it at all. Clearly, water baptism plays a declarative part in one's conversion. Yet we've also established that the act of baptism doesn't "do" or "complete" anything in and of itself.

Scripturally speaking, we must agree that one's confession must be accompanied by witnesses because this is not a "confession of sins" to God that we're talking about but rather a "proclamation to others" that we believe "Jesus is Lord" and that we are thereby pledging fealty to Him as our King.

And so this can't be done in secret. This is not accomplished in isolation. Sure, we can most certainly be alone at the moment

---

52 **Formal**. *Done in accordance with rules of convention; suitable for or constituting an official or important situation or occasion.* Encyclopedia.com (2024).

we come to believe in Jesus, be penitent, receive forgiveness, and become a child of God. And in that moment, we are certainly declared "righteous" by God, just as "Abram believed the LORD, and he credited it to him as righteousness" (Genesis 15:6, NIV). We are then justified by that faith.

But what if we never make that good confession? What if we never declare that faith to another? What if we never formally declare our loyalty to the King? Well, we now understand that without that formal declaration, one is not publicly recognized as a citizen of that kingdom. If there was no one to witness another having made that pledge, then how could anyone else in the kingdom support them if it was called into question? If one is not a member of the kingdom, he is a foreigner. He is an alien.

I know there's no circumstance today where a believer is required to present witnesses to their conversion. However, in the early Church, because of the frequent and widespread persecution many believers experienced (Acts 8:1-3), only those who had witnesses who could vouch for them would be permitted admittance into a fellowship, for safety reasons. But the principle remains. And a public, witnessed confession of faith is not easily abandoned, because our true brothers and sisters in Christ will not abandon us.

Of course, one might argue that, since God is omniscient, He "knows the heart" of a man (or woman) so that any pledge made in secret is satisfactory. Conceded, but what does it tell you about the one making the pledge if he is unwilling to make such a declaration publicly? **Is someone who is unwilling to publicly proclaim their faith really someone whose faith has overwhelmed them?** Therefore, I would argue that someone who is reluctant to make a public declaration of their faith, in some way, does not truly have faith at all.

Now, this need not be baptism, but certainly a confession in some public or witnessed way. And since baptism is already the conscripted way for Christians to make that confession, it would be silly to come up with something else.

And remember, the early Church had already established acceptable methods of baptism that could accommodate those who were infirm and unable to get to a body of water to do this. So that if one was unable to get baptized, we got you covered (wink). However, criticism remains for those who are unwilling to get baptized.

Alternatively, since baptism on its own is meaningless, one who professes faith and receives baptism, and yet is not repentant, accomplishes nothing but getting wet. Ultimately, that baptism only serves as a declaration of self-worship and condemnation, since its purpose is only public acceptance.[53]

But what about the Holy Spirit? Does He come to us when we first believe, or only after our profession of that faith through baptism or other declaration that Jesus is Lord? While Paul makes it clear to us that we are justified and saved when we have come to true faith and repentance—whether or not we have the opportunity to declare that faith publicly—there is no clarity about when the gift of the Spirit comes upon us.

It's here that one could speculate that the Holy Spirit does not come until after our public confession. While one is saved and justified by faith, one's ongoing sanctification—through which one is transformed to be more like Jesus—is only accomplished by the Holy Spirit. For many who believe initially, as Jesus explains in His parable of the sower, their faith may not persist because "they had no root" or, perhaps, they had not yet received the Holy Spirit.

> *"Listen then to what the parable of the sower means: When anyone hears the message about the kingdom and does not understand it, the evil one comes and snatches away what was sown in their heart. This is the seed sown along the path. The*

---

53   Ironically, false baptisms seldom occur outside of Western society. In many other parts of the world, confessing faith in Christ is considered abhorrent, especially in Jewish or Muslim cultures, causing separation from family and friends, and in some places even criminalized, with believers being imprisoned, tortured, and/or murdered, just as in the days of the early Church.

> *seed falling on rocky ground refers to someone who hears the word and at once receives it with joy. But since they have no root, they last only a short time. When trouble or persecution comes because of the word, they quickly fall away. The seed falling among the thorns refers to someone who hears the word, but the worries of this life and the deceitfulness of wealth choke the word, making it unfruitful. But the seed falling on good soil refers to someone who hears the word and understands it. This is the one who produces a crop, yielding a hundred, sixty or thirty times what was sown."*
>
> MATTHEW 13:18-23 NIV

Everyone has their own spiritual journey, and one can really only judge for themselves. However, believers who have undergone faithful baptism seem more likely to grow in their faith and display lasting changes than those who have either not been baptized, did so without repentance, or were under duress or coercion. Such lasting changes also may have much to do with believers undergoing baptism as a "rite of passage" in much the same way as Jews passing through the ceremony of the *bar-mitzvah*, where adolescents become "children of the law." Such rites of passage in any culture strengthen and solidify a youth's cultural perspective, and they are more inclined to stay connected to that culture than those who do not undergo such a rite, yet only when it is accompanied by faith.

GET YOUR BLESSED HANDS OFF ME!

> *When the apostles in Jerusalem heard that Samaria had accepted the word of God, they sent Peter and John to Samaria. When they arrived, they prayed for the new believers there that they might receive the Holy Spirit, because the Holy Spirit had not yet come on any of them; they had simply been baptized in the name of the Lord Jesus. Then Peter and John*

placed their hands on them, and they received the Holy Spirit.
Acts 8:14-17 NIV

Oh, so I guess maybe one *doesn't* receive the Holy Spirit at baptism? In this passage, we see that there were Samaritans (not all of them) who had accepted the gospel. We've established that this was only step one. Then it says that the Holy Spirit hadn't come because the Samaritans "had simply been baptized in the name of Jesus." Step two. Hmm.

They accepted the gospel message and they made the decision to get baptized in the name of Jesus (not John or somebody else). What did they do wrong? And how did Peter and John even know that they hadn't yet received the Spirit? These are good questions, I know, but ones to which I have no answers. The Bible simply says what it says, so anything else here is speculation.

So let's speculate, shall we?

Well, there are some churches that teach that this passage "clearly" indicates that the Holy Spirit does not come until the laying on of hands, citing Acts 19:1-6 as additional evidence for this. But if we extrapolate this a bit, we must then be concerned with the qualifications of those who were making the transfer. If the Holy Spirit was given through touch only, then it would seem there must be a *chain of custody* concern. Surely only the original apostles from Pentecost had been given the Spirit, so only they had the power to transfer that gift to others!

And if that were true, then every recipient that followed would be able (and probably be required) to trace their spiritual lineage all the way back to a specific apostle. Following that logic, the Church could not possibly have exploded as it did because of all the required recordkeeping that would be necessary during the process. And if that were the case, then which apostle got credit for the three thousand on Pentecost (officially speaking)?

> *Then Ananias went to the house and entered it. Placing his hands on Saul, he said, "Brother Saul, the Lord—Jesus, who appeared to you on the road as you were coming here—has sent me so that you may see again and be filled with the Holy Spirit." Immediately, something like scales fell from Saul's eyes, and he could see again. He got up and was baptized, and after taking some food, he regained his strength.*
>
> Acts 9:17-19 NIV

Even the apostle Paul's receiving of the Holy Spirit here would have to be questioned, since he came in contact only with a man named Ananias. How can we know for sure that Ananias had been touched personally by an apostle? Moreover, how could the now apostle Paul have equal standing with the apostle Peter?

And Peter, when speaking to his fellow Jewish disciples in Jerusalem, explains that it is, in fact, God that bestows the Holy Spirit upon the believer:

> *While Peter was still speaking these words, the Holy Spirit came on all who heard the message. The circumcised believers who had come with Peter were astonished that the gift of the Holy Spirit had been poured out even on Gentiles. For they heard them speaking in tongues and praising God.*
>
> *Then Peter said, "Surely no one can stand in the way of their being baptized with water. They have received the Holy Spirit just as we have." [54] So he ordered that they be baptized in the name of Jesus Christ. Then they asked Peter to stay with them for a few days.*
>
> Acts 10:44-47 NLT

So why did some receive the Spirit and others didn't? Why, in some cases, were these extra steps involved? Or why, in this

---

54   Peter saw the Holy Spirit come upon these believers, and seeing these Gentile believers speaking in tongues was definitive evidence that they'd received the Holy Spirit too. See https://www.bibleref.com/Acts/11/Acts-11-17.html

last example, did the Holy Spirit fall upon these new believers even before they got baptized? Well, this seems to clearly be a great example of the "mystery of God" proclaimed throughout the New Testament.[55]

This question of "when" the Holy Spirit comes was foundational to my studying of this subject in the first place. I'd honestly hoped to nail it down through a careful examination of the Scriptures. Unfortunately, all the examples we have available to us took place during the time of the apostles—and by the apostles. And the mechanisms God chose to employ the Holy Spirit during the early days of the Church, as well as the methods through which He imparted the Spirit to believers, seemed to have varied greatly. As a result, contemporary Christians would be hard-pressed to identify any specific method that applies today.

In the end, the bulk of the available text indicates that the Holy Spirit was received upon belief in Jesus. Period. There was no delay whatsoever. That which took place in Samaria and the other exceptional examples were just that: exceptions. They were not the norm for New Testament believers and would not appear to be required for us today. God is the "gift" giver, and so the timing of that event is ultimately up to Him. We can only be assured that He will certainly give us His Spirit as a lasting symbol of His covenant with us, and as a lasting power that we may grow into obedience and confidence in all that He promises.

---

55   *The Mystery of God.* See Ephesians 3:4, Colossians 2:2, Colossians 4:3, Revelation 10:7, and others.

The Fruit of Repentance
Chapter 14: No Looking Back

Then John went from place to place on both sides of the Jordan River, preaching that people should be baptized to show that they had repented of their sins and turned to God to be forgiven . . . When the crowds came to John for baptism, he said, "You brood of snakes! Who warned you to flee the coming wrath? Prove by the way you live that you have repented of your sins and turned to God. Don't just say to each other, 'We're safe, for we are descendants of Abraham.' That means nothing, for I tell you, God can create children of Abraham from these very stones. Even now the ax of God's judgment is poised, ready to sever the roots of the trees. Yes, every tree that does not produce good fruit will be chopped down and thrown into the fire."

Luke 3:3, 7-9 NLT

OVER THE PREVIOUS THOUSAND YEARS, the Jewish community (Israel) had gone through a number of major ups and downs. There were seasons when the nation worshiped God, and seasons when they had fallen far away from Him. When the nation was united with God, there were always those who lived among them who were neither Jewish nor who worshiped God. Likewise, when the nation had fallen away from God and practiced idolatry and followed none of the laws of Moses, there were always those who lived among them who remained faithful to God and sought to honor Him with their lives.

It was, has been, and is no different for the Christian nation than for the Jewish one. In both cases, there are many who claim to be "children of God" (Christians) or "children of Abraham" (Jews) who claim this in name only, as they have not devoted themselves (set themselves apart) for God's honor.

In the passage above, John son of Zechariah serves as a prophet, speaking the words of God to prepare the people for the coming Messiah, his cousin Jesus (Luke 1:24-28). John says to the crowd, "Don't assume your salvation is secure simply because you were born into the family of Israel. It is not your parents' faith nor your lineage that makes you 'righteous.' God is already prepared to cut you off and throw you into the fire unless you repent and begin to bear the fruit that comes as a by-product of living according to the ways of God" (Luke 3:7-9, *paraphrased*).

John's message to his listeners was clear: produce fruit in keeping with repentance. For when we are regularly penitent and continue to demonstrate the desire to live according to God's standard, we will be rewarded. There is nothing we can do to get right or stay right with God, of course. Only Jesus' atonement on the cross could do that. But in response to that gift of a new life in Christ, we generate an outward manifestation of a changed heart.

> *"Each tree is recognized by its own fruit. People do not pick figs from thornbushes, or grapes from briers."*
> Luke 6:44 NIV

> *"Remain in me, as I also remain in you. No branch can bear fruit by itself; it must remain in the vine. Neither can you bear fruit unless you remain in me."*
> John 15:4 NIV

So, if we acknowledge only that we are sinful by nature, yet do not express our desire to change by inviting the Holy Spirit to work inside to change us, then the net outcome is that there is no change. Sure, we can attend church, volunteer, attend Bible studies and small groups, but we will not really be open to the changes necessary to bring us to salvation. For then it is only with our own mouths we have *declared ourselves* righteous, having failed to offer our own lives as living sacrifices, so that we never bear any fruit.

When one lives this way, her proclaimed "faith" is simply nothing more than a misguided effort to belong to another social club. And it is this so-called "believer" who lives the same sinful lifestyle she always has, having no desire nor feeling any compulsion to change her ways. And it is this "Christian" that all non-believers hold up as evidence of the hypocrisy of Christianity, and proof that being a Christian is meaningless.

> *"But when the king came in to see the guests [at the Wedding Banquet], he noticed a man there who was not wearing wedding clothes. He asked, 'How did you get in here without wedding clothes, friend?' The man was speechless. Then the king told the attendants, 'Tie him hand and foot, and throw him outside, into the darkness, where there will be weeping and gnashing of teeth.' For many are invited, but few are chosen."*
>
> MATTHEW 22:11-14 NIV

John preached that God called him to baptize people with water to "prepare the way for the Lord, make straight paths for him (Luke 3:4b)." As we've been discussing, baptism with water was one of the Jewish components of one's conversion to Judaism. Here John indicates that this water would be a baptism of repentance, signifying one's decision to change direction and begin following God's ways. Remember, John's audience were already Jews, and this was not a purification ritual. But those who heard John's message of repentance and forgiveness by God for their waywardness responded by allowing themselves to be submerged in the Jordan River.

Again, there was nothing magical about that muddy river, but the transformation that occurred in every heart—that decided to repent and demonstrate that repentance through baptism—was nothing short of miraculous. For just as Christ's resurrection was miraculous, so is the resurrection of every individual who has died to themselves through repentance and baptism.

> *Or have you forgotten that when we were joined with Christ Jesus in baptism, we joined him in his death? For we died and were buried with Christ by baptism. And just as Christ was raised from the dead by the glorious power of the Father, now we also may live new lives.*
>
> Romans 6:3-4 NLT

The apostle Paul addresses the lack of repentance in his letter to the believers in Rome. This book in the New Testament is required reading for every believer, and Paul walks through responses to several typical arguments many make in regard to having to "perform" or do "good works" as a Christian. Many would argue, since they have been "saved" through Christ and can neither earn their way to heaven nor lose their salvation, why should they bother being obedient to Christ? If they're forgiven, why can't they just do what they want since they are now "free in Christ"?

While the entirety of the book of Romans covers a wide variety of such arguments, Paul addresses those who feel they are justified—just as John did to his hearers—by simply being circumcised (as a Jew) or baptized (as a Christian):

> *Circumcision has value if you observe the law, but if you break the law, you have become as though you had not been circumcised. So then, if those who are not circumcised keep*

160

the law's requirements, will they not be regarded as though they were circumcised? The one who is not circumcised physically and yet obeys the law will condemn you who, even though you have the written code and circumcision, are a lawbreaker. A person is not a Jew who is one only outwardly, nor is circumcision merely outward and physical.

ROMANS 2:25-28 NIV

Paul makes clear that circumcision, like baptism, is meaningless if you continue to live your life in opposition to God's commandments. And as John said, just because you were circumcised or baptized as a baby, that does not have any bearing on how you live your life—unless you allow it to. It is not our parents who determine our faith and right standing with God, though they may hopefully influence it.

Our righteousness comes through our own faith, not the faith of others. Only when we are old enough to understand what sin is can we truly choose repentance and accept the life of freedom in the One who gives it.

Well then, am I suggesting that the law of God is sinful? Of course not! In fact, it was the law that showed me my sin. I would never have known that coveting is wrong if the law had not said, "You must not covet." But sin used this command to arouse all kinds of covetous desires within me! If there were no law, sin would not have that power. At one time I lived without understanding the law. But when I learned the command not to covet, for instance, the power of sin came to life, and I died.

So I discovered that the law's commands, which were supposed to bring life, brought spiritual death instead. Sin took advantage of those commands and deceived me; it used the commands to kill me. But still, the law itself is holy, and its commands are holy and right and good. But how can that be? Did the law, which is good, cause my death? Of course not! Sin used what was good to bring about my condemnation to death. So we can see how terrible sin really is. It uses God's

> *good commands for its own evil purposes.*
> ROMANS 7:7-13 NLT

To answer the obvious question, those children who die before they become aware of the consequences of sin (not to be confused with knowing right and wrong), and those who are born with mental disabilities that prevent them from being able to understand sin, God considers them as innocent. Since God is just, it would be illogical and unjust for Him to punish those who are incapable of acknowledging their sin. But the question ultimately is not about others and all those special circumstances. The question is, "What about me?" Have I done anything more than simply accept the gospel with joy and allow it to have no significant impact on my life? Or have I not only proclaimed "Jesus is Lord" but also *made* Him my Lord?

> *"The seed that fell on good soil represents those who truly hear and understand God's word and produce a harvest of thirty, sixty, or even a hundred times as much as had been planted!"*
> MATTHEW 13:23 NLT

For only when we truly hear and understand God's Word, and allow it to cut our hearts and compel us to repentance, will we produce fruit in keeping with that repentance.

> *When the crowd heard [Peter's message], they were deeply troubled. They said to Peter and the other apostles, "Brothers, what should we do?" Peter replied, "Change your hearts and lives. Each of you must be baptized in the name of Jesus Christ for the forgiveness of your sins. Then you will receive the gift of the Holy Spirit."*
> ACTS 2:37-38 CEB

And what does this fruit look like? How might our lives reflect this "turning towards God?" Well, Paul explains it like this:

> *Now the works of the flesh are obvious: sexual immorality, impurity, depravity, idolatry, sorcery, hostilities, strife, jealousy, outbursts of anger, selfish rivalries, dissensions, factions, envying, murder, drunkenness, carousing, and similar things. I am warning you, as I had warned you before: Those who practice such things will not inherit the kingdom of God!*
>
> *But the fruit of the Spirit is love, joy, peace, patience, kindness, goodness, faithfulness, gentleness, and self-control. Against such things there is no law. Now those who belong to Christ have crucified the flesh with its passions and desires. If we live by the Spirit, let us also behave in accordance with the Spirit.*
>
> GALATIANS 5:19-25 NET

The author of 1 John puts it this way:

> *And we can be sure that we know him if we obey his commandments. If someone claims, "I know God," but doesn't obey God's commandments, that person is a liar and is not living in the truth. But those who obey God's word truly show how completely they love him. That is how we know we are living in him. Those who say they live in God should live their lives as Jesus did.*
>
> 1 JOHN 2:3-6 NLT

Those who say they live in God should live their lives as Jesus did. As we embrace the changes the Spirit brings, and allow Him to move and work inside of us without restriction, we begin to experience those "fruits" of the Spirit, and discover how easy and rewarding it is to give that fruit away to others.

The Obedience of Faith

Chapter 15: Being Part of the Miracle

OUR SINFUL NATURE IS A VICIOUS CIRCLE: what we think affects how we feel, which affects how we behave, which affects how we perceive the world around us, which affects how we think.

Moreover, "who" we spend the most time with has the greatest influence on "what" we think! So if your greatest source of input is a liberal or conservative news program, you will be constrained to that viewpoint, as in an echo chamber. If you spend your free time watching videos, you will be significantly influenced by the content you are watching. For social media users, are we not force-fed "recommended" content similar to what we're already watching?

Without the truth, and without purpose and the support of others to help you stay upright, you are at the mercy of the wind, and you will bend and grow in whatever direction it is blowing.

But if you want to be successful at something, you will find others who are successful at that something and do what *they* do. Whether that's watching specific videos, reading books, attending seminars, or connecting personally with such individuals, you must spend as much time with them as you can, "apprenticing" under them and studying to become a master.

But because God does not "make" us do anything we are unwilling to do (what do we call that again?), the Holy Spirit is powerless unless and until we remove His "safety protocols" and allow Him to work freely within us. Then the work the Holy

Spirit performs is the changing of our hearts and renewing of our minds (Romans 12:2) so that the outward expressions of those internal changes manifest themselves in a new way of living.

When we're ready to let God change us, we need to make a change. We must spend more time listening to God's instruction (God's Word), spending time with Him in prayer, and being open to the suggestions the Spirit makes to us on the fly. We must do everything we can to surround ourselves with other believers who are pursuing the same "success." We must continue to attend a local church, as we're instructed:

> *Don't stop meeting together with other believers, which some people have gotten into the habit of doing. Instead, encourage each other, especially as you see the day drawing near.*
> HEBREWS 10:25 CEB

Through this process, we discover God's faithfulness as we become witnesses to our own transformation. We quickly recognize God's intimate involvement in our day-to-day living, and we grow encouraged to take even larger, riskier leaps of faith—leaving our comfort zones and pursuing "even greater things" (John 1:50).

To me, this brings images of a scene in the final act of *Indiana Jones and the Last Crusade*.[56] You remember the scene: Indy is navigating the treacherous "tests" leading to the final resting place of the Holy Grail. The final test in that sequence is the "leap from the lion's mouth." As Indy stands at the precipice of the gaping darkness of death, he recognizes this challenge as being a "leap of faith." Willing to risk his own life for that of his father's (who lies dying in the outer chamber), Indy closes his eyes and steps out in faith.

It is in that moment that "his faith has saved him," as his foot

---

56   *Indiana Jones and the Last Crusade.* Lucasfilm and Paramount Pictures (1989).

lands firmly on the stone bridge that was not visible to him previously. Had he allowed his fear to rule, he would not have taken that step to retrieve the cup of "living water" that ultimately saved his father's life, his own, and the friends with him.

TAKE A GIANT LEAP

Obedience comes in different shapes and forms, and those that follow blindly are often criticized for doing so. In the military, past and present, disobeying a direct order was and is cause for imprisonment or execution. But in war and in everyday life, many have been emotionally and spiritually destroyed by their own decision to follow orders that contradicted their moral positions. They did what they were told, instead of doing what was right.

In many cases, obedience is "acting in good faith" that the command or instruction given is morally sound, has a good purpose, and will produce the desired outcome. Good faith is also rooted in the confidence in the one issuing the command. You cannot act in good faith if the one who commands you demonstrates no trustworthiness or has shown bad judgment in the past. Most folks will not obey one who shows bad moral character, unless they consider themselves of similar ilk.

Blind faith, in contrast, has those of us following, repeating, or even arguing and fighting for someone or something without any understanding of its source or character. Many hear false stories or are given bad information they believe to be true, and will cheerfully spread it to others as if from their own experiences. I've met some who seem willing to die on the hill of a falsehood they've accepted as true because they trusted its source, even though that source had done nothing to earn that trust. (Those sources are typically the echo chambers I mentioned earlier.)

Following Jesus is definitely *not* blind faith. And it is far more than just good faith. When Jesus comes down to meet us where we're at, He makes an impression on us by demonstrating His love for us in doing so. Because Jesus is actively pursuing us from day one, we know the One whom we follow. We may not fully trust Him at first, being unwilling to completely submit to His authority. But over time—more for some than others—we gain the opportunity to witness God working personally in our lives. As a result, just like Abraham, we find it easier and easier to hear and obey.

And the apostle Peter instructs us to always be prepared to explain why we believe (1 Peter 3:15) when someone asks. As new believers, our testimony regarding how we came to Jesus is often all we have to offer, for we have not yet learned all the truths and lessons contained in God's Word or from the salty nuggets that tumble out of the mouths of other brothers and sisters in Christ.

So our obedience to Christ comes from knowing the character of God. Having become familiar with God's promises and His faithfulness in keeping them, He has firmly established that He can most certainly be trusted.

The eleventh chapter of the New Testament book of Hebrews outlines a summarized history of our "faithful heroes." This book was written to Jewish believers of the day, who grew up with and were quite familiar with each of the stories and people referenced therein. The author of Hebrews uses these examples to point out how, even though they were all heroes of the faith, they had faith in a promise they knew they would not receive in their lifetimes.

> *All these people earned a good reputation because of their faith, yet none of them received all that God had promised. For God had something better in mind for us, so that they would not reach perfection without us.*
>
> HEBREWS 11:39-40 NLT

Neither have we reached perfection without *them*. Instead, we wait in joyful expectation for the last day on which we will all be

168

raised up together in new life. In the meantime, we continue to live in faithful obedience to God and His Word.

NO SHORTCUTS

Who doesn't like a good shortcut? Sometimes, my impatience will cause me to drive longer distances to keep me from sitting in traffic. How much more do we love passing gently through a green light than having to stop at a red one? We all hate waiting, and we despise lines even more. Of course, because of our slothfulness, we'll endure the drive-thru lines at In-and-Out, Chick-fil-A, and Starbucks! And while we may say we're "thankful" to have online shopping, we are now accustomed to receiving everything we buy online the very next day. Anything later is simply unacceptable.

We've already seen how Noah was obedient to God and built the ark that saved him, his family, and all the land animals so that they could repopulate the earth after the flood. Later, in the Old Testament book of Exodus, we learn about the ten plagues God brought against Egypt, and the subsequent release from slavery of the Israelite people. We learn about the Passover, and the Egyptian king's final decision to let the Israelites go with Moses and Aaron to a new land flowing with milk and honey.

We read that the two million plus Israelites were required to journey together down into the Red Sea floor and walk all night long for nearly a dozen miles while the sea raged to their right and to their left. And we know that just as the last member of the group stepped up onto the opposite shore, God released the sea back into its place to swallow up the Egyptian army that pursued them.

The Israelites did not know where they were going, yet they were obedient to God and did as He commanded them through Moses. God did not have to play it out that way, did He? He could have just snatched up His people and set them down somewhere else, Star Trek style. He could have erased the Egyptians' memories and had them forget the Israelites were ever even there.

But instead, God commanded the people to make the effort. Or, more appropriately, He had them participate in their own salvation. He didn't want pawns to control, He wanted followers, a kingdom of people who would trust in Him and rely on Him for those things they could not do on their own. So, He didn't shortcut any of that process. In fact, He caused them to walk for over twenty days before they even reached the Red Sea crossing. At one point, He actually caused them to travel back the way they came for a bit. But all of this had a purpose. He wanted the people to see Him acting on their behalf. He was creating an opportunity for them to trust Him a little bit more.

> *Now the LORD spoke to Moses, saying, "Tell the sons of Israel to turn back and camp before Pi-hahiroth, between Migdol and the sea; you shall camp in front of Baal-zephon, opposite it, by the sea. For Pharaoh will say of the sons of Israel, 'They are wandering aimlessly in the land; the wilderness has shut them in.' Thus I will harden Pharaoh's heart, and he will chase after them; and I will be honored through Pharaoh and all his army, and the Egyptians will know that I am the LORD." And they did so.*
>
> EXODUS 14:1-4 NASB

NO MAGIC WAND

A few hundred years later (or just turn your Bible to 2 Kings 5), we learn about a man named Naaman. Now Naaman was a mighty warrior and commander of the Aramean army (modern-day Syria). That nation's king had great admiration for Naaman because of his battlefield prowess, but unfortunately, during one of his recent campaigns, Naaman had contracted leprosy.

> *At this time Aramean raiders had invaded the land of Israel,
> and among their captives was a young girl who had been
> given to Naaman's wife as a maid. One day the girl said to her
> mistress, "I wish my master would go to see the prophet in
> Samaria. He would heal him of his leprosy."*
>
> 2 KINGS 5:2-3 NLT

Naaman was not an Israelite, of course, but since there was
no cure for leprosy, the girl's urging gave him a glimmer of hope
where he otherwise had none. So, with permission from his
king, he journeyed to Israel, ultimately landing at the doorstep
of Elisha, the prophet of God who was well known throughout
the land.

> *So Naaman went with his horses and chariots and waited at
> the door of Elisha's house. But Elisha sent a messenger out to
> him with this message: "Go and wash yourself seven times in
> the Jordan River. Then your skin will be restored, and you will
> be healed of your leprosy."*
>
> *But Naaman became angry and stalked away. "I thought
> he would certainly come out to meet me!" he said. "I expected
> him to wave his hand over the leprosy and call on the name of
> the LORD his God and heal me! Aren't the rivers of Damascus,
> the Abana and the Pharpar, better than any of the rivers of
> Israel? Why shouldn't I wash in them and be healed?" So
> Naaman turned and went away in a rage.*
>
> 2 KINGS 5:9-12 NLT

Naaman was furious because he was looking for a quick wave
of Elisha's hand for healing. His stature gave him a bit of pride,
and he was unwilling, at first, to "do" something to be healed.
Moreover, because of that same pride, he was frustrated that
Elisha did not show him the respect of coming out to meet him.

"I expected him to wave his hand and heal me," he says.
"What's the logic in going down to the dirty river of the Jordan

and getting wet?" He figured he could have done that in one of the cleaner rivers closer to home if that's what it took. Why was he being told to jump through these hoops?

Well, God wanted Naaman to learn to "trust the process." As Jesus often said, "Your faith has healed you." As we continue to learn, it is not our actions themselves that bring change or healing to us and others. But when we are obedient, even though we usually don't understand the "why", God will bless our efforts simply because we trusted Him enough to act in that faith.

For it is our faith that brings us to a place of *willingness* to obey, but it is our action that *demonstrates* our obedience. **For until we act, there is nothing of substance that affects change.**

> *But a woman who had been suffering from a hemorrhage for twelve years came up behind him and touched the edge of his cloak. For she kept saying to herself, "If only I touch his cloak, I will be healed." But when Jesus turned and saw her he said, "Have courage, daughter! Your faith has made you well." And the woman was healed from that hour.*
>
> MATTHEW 9:20-22 NET

In this example, the woman wasn't healed because she touched Jesus' cloak. She was healed because she *believed* touching His cloak would heal her. As He says, "Your faith has healed you." But her healing didn't happen *until* she reached out and touched His cloak. It was indeed her faith in Jesus that brought healing, but nothing would have changed if she hadn't had the courage and the fortitude to fight the crowd and make it happen!

It is this kind of faith that Elisha is demanding of Naaman. Yes, God could certainly heal Naaman instantly, no faith required. But the purpose of any miracle was to bring glory to God and draw others to Him. If Naaman hadn't needed to do anything for healing, he could have later convinced himself that he just got better, with no real evidence that God was involved.

And more importantly, Naaman's faith was lacking. He was effectively saying that he did not believe Elisha had the power of God to heal him. At this point, if he goes out to the river and washes and nothing happens, he will look like a fool for having had blind faith and jumping not once, but seven times, into the muddy Jordan River.

> *But his officers tried to reason with him and said, "Sir, if the prophet had told you to do something very difficult, wouldn't you have done it? So you should certainly obey him when he says simply, 'Go and wash and be cured!'" So Naaman went down to the Jordan River and dipped himself seven times, as the man of God had instructed him. And his skin became as healthy as the skin of a young child, and he was healed!*
>
> 2 KINGS 5:13-14 NLT

But surely, it was not the Jordan River that held any special properties. Surely, it was not that he dipped himself seven times in it.[57]

Now, I know what you're going to say: *Don't call me Shirley!* So instead, let me be frank. What healed Naaman here, and what healed the woman mentioned in Matthew 9, was the demonstrated faith that we like to call . . . obedience.

Naaman positioned himself where he could allow God to work. Naaman brought himself to the point of humiliation, to demonstrate his faith in God's ability to heal him by simply doing the very thing he was commanded to do. By acting in faith, he showed God that he was ready to be healed.

So often we ask God to do something grand and miraculous in our lives. But we expect Him to just wave His magic wand and do it. However, most of the time, **God will not act until we put**

---

57   Seven wasn't a magic number, though it was special. This number communicated a sense of "fullness" or "completeness." The first example appears in Genesis 2:2, as God rested from the process of creation on the seventh day, not because He was tired, but because His work was complete! This makes sense of the pervasive appearance of "sevens" in Scripture.

ourselves in a position to participate in the miracle.

All Washed Up
An Epilogue

So why get baptized? Well, perhaps this discussion has raised more questions than it's answered. Maybe, after looking at the variety of ways in which people in the early Church came to faith, experienced baptism, and received the Holy Spirit, it seems even less important that one be baptized.

Well, when I was younger, many tried to convince me that I must be baptized, as it was "definitely" a part of the salvation process. So much so, that some churches demand your re-baptism when joining *their* church, so that they can be sure it's legitimate. They don't want you going through life thinking you'd done it right, only to discover on the Last Day that you belonged to the wrong church.

I mentioned at the start how I felt it important to work out the details of this subject because of all the confusion out there. I wanted to be able to talk plainly and confidently about it, removing those nagging questions from my own mind regarding the details. Up to the point of talking this all over with you, I was left only with my own ideas and conclusions, taken from the many words of other people over the years. Sure, I'd read all these same Scriptures before, but their varying details caused the subject to remain unclear. I'd never allowed myself to take the time, until now, to really pore over them.

But having now done so, and especially with all your wonderful and diverse input, I can now confidently allow those different events, as they're recorded in the book of Acts, to simply be . . . special.

My problem before was (and for many others it still is) the desire to reconcile those differences as part of a larger common and contemporary practice. Because we must look at God's Word as unchanging and always relevant, we often ignore the cultural and circumstantial context of the text. While the precepts are always applicable, it does not necessarily follow that the details are.

Remember that the apostles were imbued with special powers of the Holy Spirit. They were given those powers to accomplish special things for God's glory at that special time. It does not follow that all disciples everywhere for all time had or have the gifts of healing, prophecy, speaking in tongues, or the laying on of hands to impart the Spirit to others.

We no longer live in tents or wander the Middle Eastern desert. We don't offer animal sacrifices to pay for our wrongdoings. We're not concerned with our patrilineal heritage, and we never bother to wash the feet of our guests, even when we may demand they take off their shoes before entering our home. Women wear pants, and men wear dresses, and the lines that have long-since distinguished one from the other continue to blur.

However, we have certainly read together the context of all these examples of washing, purification, and baptism. We've seen how many unusual situations occurred in the early Church that excited and confused the apostles then, so why should we expect such clarity now? Everything was being made new, and they just rolled with it. The Holy Spirit seemed to be making it up as He went along—even though He certainly knew what He was doing—and the apostles were simply obedient to His direction.

And that's where we should land as well. Like the crowd of 3,000 at Pentecost, and the Ethiopian eunuch with whom Philip shared the gospel, we must respond. As Naaman was instructed to immerse himself in the Jordan for cleansing, and Jacob's household discarded their pasts for a new future, we must respond.

The Israelites died to their previous lives of slavery in Egypt and were born again into their new lives as children of God by passing through the Red Sea. God washed away their previous master of slavery and made them slaves of righteousness. He put His seal of approval on them before they had ever done anything to make themselves worthy of such approval.

> *But God demonstrates his own love for us in this: While we were still sinners, Christ died for us.*
> ROMANS 5:8 NIV

It was and is expected that everyone who claims to follow Christ respond to the gospel by allowing the Spirit to transform them from the inside, which then expresses itself outwardly. The apostle Paul addressed the ridiculous notion that one could choose to continue living their old lives simply because they were covered by Jesus' blood. He explained:

> *Well then, should we keep on sinning so that God can show us more and more of his wonderful grace? Of course not! Since we have died to sin, how can we continue to live in it? Or have you forgotten that when we were joined with Christ Jesus in baptism, we joined him in his death? For we died and were buried with Christ by baptism. And just as Christ was raised from the dead by the glorious power of the Father, now we also may live new lives.*
> ROMANS 6:1-4 NLT

Again, the assumption is that the believer *has* undergone baptism. There is no ambiguity here. And Paul explains that it is through baptism that we are "united" with Jesus in His death, the very death that frees us from our slavery to sin. And while this action is certainly symbolic, as we've seen, this exercise in humility demonstrates the power of God at work within us, and our willingness to allow Him to work. It must not be ignored!

We've examined the beginnings of circumcision and why it had such value. As a result, we can now understand its cultural significance and how it corresponded to a greater sense of belonging to the community. And this understanding really connects the dots for us in how baptism relates to a greater sense of belonging to the body of Christ.

Hopefully, you've come to truly understand the value of discipleship, or apprenticeship, and see how baptism serves as an expression of commitment and fealty to the one true King.

And through all our investigation, we should now be confident that our salvation is based entirely on our faith, and not on any secondary actions. We were powerless before to bring ourselves to salvation, and we most certainly don't have what it takes to maintain it, nor is it within our power to lose it!

We know that it is the Holy Spirit working in and through us that purifies us and prepares us for eternity, which gives us the security in knowing that there are no extra steps that need to be performed, even after death, before we can enter God's glorious presence. Jesus did all that needed doing, so nothing remains but our obedience to the Spirit and the joyful expectation of what's to come.

So then, are you still afraid of the water?

Appendix

Immersed in Conversation

The questions on the following pages are intended to stimulate small group discussion while highlighting some of the assumptions we regularly make about the world around us.

Remember, there are no wrong answers (well, there's *one*) since each of us have our own unique life experiences that carried us to this place.

Discussion questions are grouped by their relevant chapter, but feel free to ask your own. I'm not there to supervise, so have at it!

A Gentle Mist—An Introduction

1. Most of us typically accept things at face value, especially when such information comes from a trusted source. How can we know if what others tell us is the truth?

2. Discuss your first exposure to the practice of baptism.

3. The vast majority of things that we "know" do not come from personal experience and are instead received from other sources. From where do your current beliefs about baptism come?

4. Have you ever been in disagreement with something a church leader/pastor said or taught? Explain the circumstance and why you felt qualified to dispute them?

5. In *1 Peter 3:15,* the apostle Peter tells us to be able to explain the reasons for our faith. What do you think this means?

Chapter 1—Defining Baptism

Considering our preconceptions, it's quite possible that what we believe about baptism may not even be our own ideas. The purpose of this conversation is to discover the truth about what the Bible says about baptism, setting aside our preconceptions (or things we've been told) and opening ourselves up to other possibilities. We certainly may already be right, but how can we know?

1. If you haven't already, discuss where you currently land in regards to the purpose or value of baptism as a practice (this'll be fun!):

    Not Necessary at All   ← →   *Necessary for Salvation*
    | - - - - - - - - - - - - - - - - - | - - - - - - - - - - - - - - - - - |

2. In the Old Testament, the Israelites were commanded to offer regular sacrifices to atone for their sins. Do you think it's a good idea for one to get baptized regularly if they continually struggle with a particular sin?

3. Have you been baptized? If so, please share the how, the when, and the why (and discover the variations).

Chapter 2—Methods of Baptism

1. Understanding that immersion baptism was the practice of the early Church, why do you think aspersion and affusion are still used so prevalently in the orthodox (Roman Catholic, Eastern Orthodox, Anglican, etc.) churches today?

2. Discuss the idea of *original sin*.

3. While "all have sinned and fall short of God's glory," does this mean that all sin is the same in God's eyes?

4. Do we, as humans, have the power to forgive sins? And if so, do we have the right to withhold that forgiveness under certain circumstances?

Chapter 3—A Flood of Changes

1. We often talk about "picking our battles." Can you recall a time with a child (or someone else) where you just had to give up on the desired outcome because it seemed fruitless? And was the desired outcome more beneficial to them or to you?

2. Should the events recorded in Genesis be taken literally? Why or why not?

3. Did you realize that Noah's ancestors, excluding Adam, Seth, and Enoch, were all alive during Noah's lifetime? Have you ever considered the ramifications of living several hundred years? Discuss what that may have been like, pros and cons.

4. Although the account in Genesis doesn't provide any indication that Noah "preached" to the people of his day, why do you think this idea is taught so prevalently?

5. Should those who do not want God's presence in their lives be forced against their will to live in God's presence (in heaven) forever?

Chapter 4—Rebirth and Renewal

1. The Hebrew word *aron* is translated to us as "ark" which means vessel. The ark of the covenant was literally a sacred vessel where the presence of God could reside with the Israelites as they traveled. This tells us that the floating container that Noah built should be seen more as a temple or sanctuary than a boat. Read *1 Corinthians 6:18-20* and consider how it relates to the current discussion.

2. Read *Genesis 7:1-10*. God brought the various kinds of animals to Noah to load onto the ark over the seven days leading up to the Flood. Since it would have been impossible to load two of every species of animal alive at the time, what do you think the Bible means by animal "kinds"?

3. Citing this same passage, why do you think Moses notes the distinction in verse 8 between those animals "approved for eating and for sacrificing and those that were not" since the law had not yet been given and there was no such distinction?

4. Compare *Genesis 1:29-30* with *Genesis 9:1-3*. What changed?

Chapter 5—The Dead Zone

1. Perhaps you know someone who "coded" (clinical death) but was resuscitated successfully. Contrast this with Jesus' raising of Lazarus from the grave. While not the same, what does this suggest about a person's spirit after death?

2. What do you think about the idea of the dead zone?

3. In what year did the Council of Florence ratify the doctrine of purgatory?

4. Have you ever left a congregation simply because a particular pastor left or retired?

5. Why does God allow the existence of *false teachers* in the present age, and how can we know that what one teaches or preaches is not of God?

Chapter 6—Circumspect Circumstances

1. Does it pain you to learn that circumcision was already in practice before Abraham? Why do you think God mandated this procedure to "mark" His covenant with Abraham when the practice was not necessarily confined to the people of Israel?

2. When do you feel *more receptive* to God's Word? When you're in a solitary, quiet place, or when you are gathered together with other believers?

3. Share a time in your life when God demonstrated His faithfulness to you in a way that you will never forget.

4. What similarities do you see in purpose between circumcision and baptism?

Chapter 7—Washing Away the Past

1. After coming to Christ, we each immediately begin a transformation that includes the "letting go" of countless behaviors and lifestyles. While some behaviors can be discarded quickly, some remain with us for years. How can we judge other believers "progress" when we aren't witnesses to their transformation?

2. Discuss a time when you had to face a major life change that filled you with fear and anxiety. In discussing it now, do you think it was harder to embrace what was new, or to let go of the old and familiar?

3. Read *1 John 3:1-4*. What do you think it means to purify ourselves?

4. Read *Numbers 33:55*. Is there someone or something from your "old" life that you're still hanging onto? If you're willing, confess it to the group and make the decision today to *drive it out* and let it go.

Chapter 8—Changing Your Stars

1. In *Matthew 21:28-32*, Jesus tells of two brothers. Both their responses were telling of their individual character, neither of which we would praise. But with which brother do you more readily identify, whether you like it or not?

2. Watch *A Knight's Tale* if you haven't seen it! In the scene I describe where William becomes a knight, at what point do you think he actually *became* a knight?

3. Consider *Acts 11:26*. If discipleship and apprenticeship mean effectively the same thing, would you consider yourself more of a "follower" of Jesus or His "disciple"?

4. Read *Luke 14:24-26*. Considering the expectations Jesus sets here, are you gonna stick with your answer from the previous question?

Chapter 9—Can't Touch This!

1. After becoming *unclean* as a result of contact with someone else who was unclean, why do you think the "victim" would become so upset?

2. The gospels provide us with a number of times when Jesus gave healing, but why didn't He heal everyone? What was the purpose of such healing, and how does that carry over to today?

3. Although you may know that your works don't earn you a place in heaven, do you still hold a vague expectation that God will bless you in this life if you *live* a certain way?

4. Since God "makes us holy," why should we also be given the instruction to make *ourselves* holy?

Chapter 10—So Let's Keep Things Moving

1. In *Jeremiah 17:13*, God is referred to as the *mikveh* of Israel, the fountain of living water. Discuss how we can become "dried out" when we separate ourselves from God's Word.

2. Can you think of a time or situation where you believed one thing to be true, only to discover later—after opening yourself up to new ideas and new ways of thinking—that you changed that belief?

3. Discuss how God works within the "boundaries" of freewill to accomplish His plans for the future.

4. Have you ever come across a homeless person and momentarily considered what would be involved providing them with assistance beyond a quick and easy handout? What keeps us from acting on their behalf?

Chapter 11—Dirty Little Things

1. Discuss the contemporary cultural practice of removing shoes when entering a home. In what ways can this practice be self-defeating when other hygiene habits are ignored?

2. Why do you think the Church did not adopt foot-washing as a sacramental practice, such as baptism and communion?

3. Consider your thoughts and posture when you attend a church service. How much of the "world" do you bring in with you? Do you come with the hope that God will wash it all off you, or do you wash it off before you come?

4. Discuss the ways we as Christians, like the Jews, are called to stand out from the rest of the world and "be different"? Would your children or colleagues say you lean more towards "standing out" or "blending in"?

Chapter 12—Getting Wet With a Purpose

1. Have you ever been obedient to someone in authority even when you vehemently disagreed with their command?

2. Why were people coming from all over to be baptized by John? What did they believe such a baptism represented or accomplished?

3. Discuss the difference between simply "quitting" something and having true repentance. If you are willing, share a behavior you have silently stopped (or tried to stop) of which you have only recently (or perhaps never) really repented.

4. Considering what we've discussed so far about baptism and repentance, do you think one has any value without the other?

Chapter 13—Indwellable Markings

1. What is the difference between the "indwelling" and the "movement" of the Holy Spirit?

2. Given the choice, would you prefer to either have walked physically with Jesus for a short time or to enjoy the current, everyday access to Him through the Spirit (not both)?

3. Discuss your opinion on how the Spirit moved through the crowd at Pentecost. Do you think the disciples literally spoke in many different languages? Why were not all who were present able to understand the message?

4. Why do you think these folks were so willing to get baptized as a response?

Chapter 14—No Looking Back

1. Are the good works we do clear evidence of our right standing with God?

2. Does our ability to admit that "we are sinners" and that we "need Jesus" demonstrate that we are believers?

3. Does our continuing "struggle" with sin indicate that we have not been saved?

4. Many Christians have intentionally undergone baptism at a very young age, having made a "decision" to follow Jesus from early on *(likely someone in this room)*. Is there now any valid argument for them to be re-baptized or to "re-commit" their lives to Christ as adults?

Chapter 15—Being Part of the Miracle

1. What are some important reasons why Christians should remain connected with other Christians as opposed to "going it alone"?

2. When we see God acting in our lives, are we more or less inclined to take "leaps of faith" in pursuing His will for us?

3. Read *Romans 8:27-29.* Does this passage indicate that God is manipulating all things, or that He is making due with the things we give Him by our own choices?

4. Discuss a time when you asked God to act in your life or the lives of another, yet didn't witness His participation until after you acted.

All Washed Up—An Epilogue

1. What is the value of baptism? What, if anything, does it accomplish?

2. Should one who declares faith in Jesus refuse to get baptized?

3. Share one thing you learned through this whole discussion.

4. Take a look back at the first question to Chapter 1 of this discussion. Has anything changed?